Ionic Framework By Example

Build amazing cross-platform mobile apps with Ionic, the HTML5 framework that makes modern mobile application development simple

Sani Yusuf

BIRMINGHAM - MUMBAI

Ionic Framework By Example

First published: January 2016

Production reference: 1200116

Published by Packt Publishing Ltd.
Livery Place
35 Livery Street
Birmingham B3 2PB, UK.

ISBN 978-1-78528-272-0

www.packtpub.com

Credits

Author
Sani Yusuf

Reviewer
Luca Mezzalira

Commissioning Editor
Dipika Gaonkar

Acquisition Editor
Subho Gupta

Content Development Editor
Athira Laji

Technical Editor
Prajakta Mhatre

Copy Editor
Vatsal Surti

Project Coordinator
Harshal Ved

Proofreader
Safis Editing

Indexer
Rekha Nair

Graphics
Jason Monteiro

Production Coordinator
Melwyn D'sa

Cover Work
Melwyn D'sa

About the Author

Sani Yusuf is the founder of Haibrid, a company focused on creating innovative mobile solutions with hybrid technologies operating from London, England. Starting his career as a web developer, he moved on to native development of both desktop and mobile applications before developing a focus on hybrid mobile apps due to their philosophy of reusability and cross-platform operability.

When not managing his company, Sani spends his time public speaking, writing, and endlessly researching new educational and healthcare mobile solutions. Although a Nigerian by birth, Sani moved to the UK in 2010 to pursue a degree in computer science, having a great interest in healthcare and educational advancement with mobile technology.

A lover of the movie "Avatar" and a speaker of four languages, namely French, English, Arabic, and Hausa, Sani spends his free time travelling, watching movies, and watching Arsenal football club being great.

During his career, Sani has worked with companies like Anritsu, Microsoft, Huddlebuy, Envato, and more recently, Nexercise, with some of his works awarded by Microsoft, Samsung, and Aimia Ltd.

He has also written Windows Phone Beginner Series, an online tutorial series for Envato.

Acknowledgments

Firstly, I would like to thank Subho Gupta, acquisition editor of Packt Publishing, for providing me with the opportunity of writing such a wonderful book. Athira Laji, you are a gem of a unique kind for all your hard work throughout the process of writing this book. Also Luca, thanks for your kind editorial efforts.

A legendary mention of Mark Dickens, my manager while working at Anritsu, for his mentoring and great management.

A worthy mention of the people at Huddlebuy for believing in me when I pitched Ionic as a solution for their mobile needs.

I would like to recognize Alhaji Sani Nuhu Abubakar for gifting me my very first computer in 2001, a gift that would change my life forever. Also, I would love to recognize Alhaji Mohammed Ariyo, and everyone involved in helping me make conscious educational decisions. And to my kind friends Tsoma, Azeez, Anthony, Aisha B, Bhoomi, Nabeel, Samia, Sarah B, Sarah S, Sanu, Seun, and Amina. All of you gave me comfort in your own way and I appreciate it.

Massive thanks to the Ionic for building such a great framework that has changed lives. A special mention to Ryan Hana, founder of Sworkit; you empowered me to co-create Ionic UK and it is an honor to do great things with you.

Unmatched thanks to my father Alhaji Yusuf Umar, you are my everything and I am forever indebted to you. You have given me more than anyone could ever, and I will always be grateful. Mum, I will get you that mansion. Mama Maryam, I will get you that G6. Mama Saeeda, I am what I am today because of your love. Thanks to all my siblings, Maimuna, Amina, Rukaaya, Amma, Fatima, Faruq, Afrah, Chuya, and Fuad. Love you all. Thanks to all my teachers and everyone else that made this possible.

Finally, thanks to God for life and good health.

About the Reviewer

Luca Mezzalira is a passionate Italian solutions architect with more than 10 years of experience of frontend technologies, particularly in JavaScript, HTML 5, Haxe, Flash, Flex, AIR, Lua, and Swift.

He has often been involved in cutting-edge projects for mobile (iOS, Android, Blackberry,) desktop, web, TV, set top boxes, and embedded devices.

He thinks the best way to use any programming language is mastering their models. That's why he has spent a lot of time studying and researching topics like OOP, functional programming, and functional reactive programming.

With these skills, he is able to swap quite easily between different programming languages, applying the best practices learnt to drive any team to success.

He is a natural leader, delivery focused, a problem solver, and a game changer. He uses his passion on every aspect of the work, from the flow definition to the automation process.

He tries to cover every detail to improve the company standards, empower the teams, and deliver great products.

He is certified as: certified scrum master and SAFe agilist; Adobe-certified expert and instructor on Flash, Flex, AIR; Adobe community professional; and Adobe Italy consultant.

He has written for national and international technical magazines and editors. He is also a technical reviewer for Packt Publishing, Pragmatic Bookshelf, and O'Reilly.

He is a speaker for national and international conferences or community events such as O'Reilly media webinars, FullStack conference, React London UG, Scrum Gathering, Lean Kanban United Kingdom, Mobile World Congress, Flash Camp, 360 Flex, Better Software, Pycon, and so on.

In 2013, he organized an itinerant event in six different cities in Italy called "Having fun with Adobe AIR" where people learnt how to develop mobile applications for iOS, Android, and BlackBerry with Adobe AIR and Starling.

In 2015, he started the London JavaScript Community (`http://www.meetup.com/London-JavaScript-Community/`), organizing a monthly meetup event about the top "hot topics" in the JavaScript world.

The first mention is for my family that always helps me, and in particular, for my parents who support and inspire me everyday with their strength and love.

A big thanks to my brother who is also one of my best friends. He is the most clever person that I've ever met in my life; his suggestions and his ideas are so important to me.

I really have a lot of other friends to say thanks to for what we have created together until now. I hope I don't forget anybody: Piergiorgio Niero, Chiara Agazzi, Cinzia Menichelli, Francesco Bardoni, Giorgio Bianchi, Ilaria Dehò, Alessandro Bianco, Raffaella Brandoli, Mark Stanley, Frank Amankwah, Matteo Oriani, Manuele Mimo, Goy Oracha, Tommaso Magro, Sofia Faggian, Matteo Lanzi, Peter Elst, Francesca Beordo, Federico Pitone, Tiziano Fruet, Giorgio Pedergnani, Andrea Sgaravato, Fabio Bernardi, Sumi Lim, and many many others.

Last but not least, I'd like to say thanks to my girlfriend and life partner, Maela, for the amazing time we are spending together. Her passion and commitment in our relationship gives me the strength to go ahead and do my best everyday. Many thanks my love!

www.PacktPub.com

Support files, eBooks, discount offers, and more

For support files and downloads related to your book, please visit www.PacktPub.com.

Did you know that Packt offers eBook versions of every book published, with PDF and ePub files available? You can upgrade to the eBook version at www.PacktPub.com and as a print book customer, you are entitled to a discount on the eBook copy. Get in touch with us at service@packtpub.com for more details.

At www.PacktPub.com, you can also read a collection of free technical articles, sign up for a range of free newsletters and receive exclusive discounts and offers on Packt books and eBooks.

https://www2.packtpub.com/books/subscription/packtlib

Do you need instant solutions to your IT questions? PacktLib is Packt's online digital book library. Here, you can search, access, and read Packt's entire library of books.

Why subscribe?

- Fully searchable across every book published by Packt
- Copy and paste, print, and bookmark content
- On demand and accessible via a web browser

Free access for Packt account holders

If you have an account with Packt at www.PacktPub.com, you can use this to access PacktLib today and view 9 entirely free books. Simply use your login credentials for immediate access.

Table of Contents

Preface

Ionic Framework By Example is a step-by-step guide that covers the very basics of Ionic aiming to equip the reader with all the necessary knowledge needed to understand and create Ionic apps. You will start off by learning a bit about the history of Ionic, and then slowly learn to get it set up and work with its great features. You will learn to work with Ionic and create four different Ionic apps, with each app teaching you different important features of Ionic. You will also learn to connect your app to a database using Firebase. This book will also provide you with links to some great resources to further your quest for more advanced Ionic knowledge.

What this book covers

Chapter 1, First Look at Ionic, covers a brief history of Ionic and aims to make the user understand exactly what Ionic is, briefly exposing some of its features to the user. This chapter will also teach you how to set up Ionic on your computer.

Chapter 2, To-Do List App, will help the reader to create their first Ionic application, a simple to-do list application. The user will also write their very first lines of Ionic code and get to understand what an Ionic project looks like.

Chapter 3, Running Ionic Apps, equips you with the necessary knowledge of how to see your Ionic apps in action in different ways. You will run and test your app on a browser, on a mobile device using the Ionic view app, and also on a real mobile device.

Chapter 4, Ionic Components, teaches some really cool components that are part of Ionic. You will create a more advanced to-do list application that will have some Ionic components that will enable you to create some complex list items in your application.

Chapter 5, The London Tourist App, creates a new type of Ionic application. You will create an application that will hold some very cool tourist destinations in the city of London.

You will also learn to query data from a JSON resource and consume this data in your application.

Chapter 6, Advanced Ionic Components, helps the reader learn to implement some more advanced Ionic components. You will learn to implement Ionic Popover and Modal windows in your application.

Chapter 7, Customizing the App, focuses on customizing an Ionic application. The Ionic SDK comes by default with some great tools that make it easy to customize your application to fit the design guides of your brand.

Chapter 8, Building a Simple Social App, focuses on learning how to create an Ionic application that has tabs using the Ionic tabs template. You will also have a look at some of the things that make up the tabs template and learn how to add features to it.

Chapter 9, Connecting to Firebase, focuses solely on learning how to use Firebase to integrate a backend to our Ionic application. You will also be using the tabs-app that we created in *Chapter 8, Building a Simple Social App,* to learn to integrate Firebase into our application.

Chapter 10, Roundup, gives an overview of the important things that we haven't covered yet about Ionic that you might find very useful. You will also learn some useful tips about Ionic and discover some great tips on how to make even better use of Ionic to develop great apps.

What you need for this book

Firstly, you will need a Windows, Linux, or Mac computer to follow the code samples in this book. A beyond basic or intermediate knowledge of JavaScript and HTML5 is certainly essential to understand concepts discussed in this book. A basic understanding of Cordova is expected at the very least. You are expected to also have an idea of how to issue commands in a terminal window. You should also have access to a working Internet connection, and a Google account is necessary for *Chapter 9, Connecting to Firebase.*

Who this book is for

This book is aimed at individuals looking to learn how to create hybrid mobile applications with Ionic. This book is perfect for current web developers with beyond basic familiarity of HTML5 and JavaScript. AngularJS developers will also feel at home reading this book as Ionic is built with AngularJS. Native iOS and Android developers with a good understanding of HTML5 and JavaScript will also benefit highly from this book and gain knowledge on how to create hybrid mobile apps.

Conventions

In this book, you will find a number of text styles that distinguish between different kinds of information. Here are some examples of these styles and an explanation of their meaning.

Code words in text, database table names, folder names, filenames, file extensions, pathnames, dummy URLs, user input, and Twitter handles are shown as follows: "You will also notice that in your `www/lib` folder, there is a folder called `ionic` that contains all the required files to run Ionic."

A block of code is set as follows:

```
<div class="list">
    <div class="item item-input-inset">
        <label class="item-input-wrapper">
            <input type="text" placeholder="enter todo item">
        </label>
        <button class="button button-small">
            Add
        </button>
    </div>
</div>
```

Any command-line input or output is written as follows:

```
ionic serve
```

New terms and **important words** are shown in bold. Words that you see on the screen, for example, in menus or dialog boxes, appear in the text like this: "Scroll down to the **More Tools** options and select the **Developer Tools** option, as shown in the following screenshot."

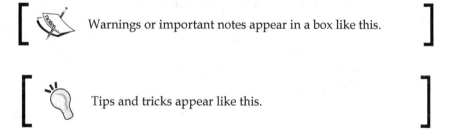

Warnings or important notes appear in a box like this.

Tips and tricks appear like this.

Reader feedback

Feedback from our readers is always welcome. Let us know what you think about this book—what you liked or disliked. Reader feedback is important for us as it helps us develop titles that you will really get the most out of.

To send us general feedback, simply e-mail feedback@packtpub.com, and mention the book's title in the subject of your message.

If there is a topic that you have expertise in and you are interested in either writing or contributing to a book, see our author guide at www.packtpub.com/authors.

Customer support

Now that you are the proud owner of a Packt book, we have a number of things to help you to get the most from your purchase.

Downloading the example code

You can download the example code files from your account at http://www.packtpub.com for all the Packt Publishing books you have purchased. If you purchased this book elsewhere, you can visit http://www.packtpub.com/support and register to have the files e-mailed directly to you.

Errata

Although we have taken every care to ensure the accuracy of our content, mistakes do happen. If you find a mistake in one of our books—maybe a mistake in the text or the code—we would be grateful if you could report this to us. By doing so, you can save other readers from frustration and help us improve subsequent versions of this book. If you find any errata, please report them by visiting http://www.packtpub.com/submit-errata, selecting your book, clicking on the **Errata Submission Form** link, and entering the details of your errata. Once your errata are verified, your submission will be accepted and the errata will be uploaded to our website or added to any list of existing errata under the Errata section of that title.

To view the previously submitted errata, go to https://www.packtpub.com/books/content/support and enter the name of the book in the search field. The required information will appear under the **Errata** section.

Piracy

Piracy of copyrighted material on the Internet is an ongoing problem across all media. At Packt, we take the protection of our copyright and licenses very seriously. If you come across any illegal copies of our works in any form on the Internet, please provide us with the location address or website name immediately so that we can pursue a remedy.

Please contact us at copyright@packtpub.com with a link to the suspected pirated material.

We appreciate your help in protecting our authors and our ability to bring you valuable content.

Questions

If you have a problem with any aspect of this book, you can contact us at questions@packtpub.com, and we will do our best to address the problem.

1
First Look at Ionic

Before we begin this book, it is very important that we understand just exactly what we are dealing with. The best way to understand this is by having a short history on mobile development, in general, and understand how tools like Ionic help mobile developers create beautiful mobile apps.

The beginning

The year 2006 saw the beginning of the smartphone era with the launch of the iPhone by Apple. By 2008, Google had launched its answer to Apple's iOS operating system. This new operating system was called **Android**, and by 2010, it was clear that smartphones running iOS and Android dominantly covered the mobile ecosystem. Fast forward to today, the dominance of iOS and Android is not so different even though Windows for mobile by Microsoft has made some gains on the mobile front. It is fair to say that Android, iOS, and Windows make up the majority of the ecosystem with the first two at the forefront by a large margin.

The launch of the smartphone era also gave birth to the concept of mobile applications. Mobile apps are the medium by which we deliver and obtain most of our content on mobile phones. They are great and everyone with a smartphone pretty much has a number of apps downloaded on their devices to perform specific actions or achieve specific goals. This was massive for developers, and the software vendors also provided tools that enabled developers to create their own third-party mobile apps for users. We refer to these applications, built using the tools provided by the software vendors, as **native mobile applications**.

The problem

As great as mobile apps are, there is a small problem with how they are developed. Firstly, for each mobile development platform, the software vendor provides its own unique set of tools to build applications for its platforms. We know these tools as SDKs. The following table shows how each platform differs in terms of tools and SDK options to create native mobile apps for their ecosystems:

Operating system	SDK	Programming language
iOS	iOS SDK	Objective-C/Swift
Android	Android SDK	JAVA
Windows for mobile	Windows SDK	.NET

To make a clear statement, we are not trying to downplay the use of native tools. As noted earlier, native tools are great but come with a great cost and time constraint. Firstly, you are unable to build the same app for different platforms with the same set of tools. For the Android version of your app, you will need a team of skilled android developers. For the iOS version of your app, you will need a team of Objective-C or Swift developers to create the iOS version of the same app. Also, there is no code sharing between these two teams, meaning that a feature developed on one platform will have to be completely developed on the other platform again. This is highly inefficient in terms of development and very time consuming.

Another problem is that because you are hiring two separate teams that are completely independent of one another even though they are both trying to create the same thing, you are left with a growing cost. For example, if you decided you wanted to create a Windows for mobile version of your mobile app, you will need to recruit another team of .NET developers and they will have to build everything present on the other existing platforms from scratch since they cannot reuse any of the already built tools.

For a company like Facebook, which makes revenue in the billions, it might make sense to go down the native path as cost and talent for native development would probably not be a part of their concern. However, for the most part, not everyone building or trying to build a mobile app is a company like Facebook. Most people want to get a simple, great, powerful app out there as quick as possible. Furthermore, some of these people want to use their preexisting skill set to build apps for multiple platforms without having to learn new programming languages.

Before mobile applications, web apps ruled the world for the most part. We had more people developing for the web technologies consisting mostly of HTML, CSS, and JavaScript. One great thing we got used to with the web was that it was platform independent. This meant that as long as you had a browser application on any device, you were able to interact with any web application without any problem.

So when mobile apps came, it was a big change for most web developers because with mobile apps, each platform was self-dependent, and apps made for one platform would not work for another platform.

Apache Cordova

Apache Cordova is a technology that lets any web application be packaged as a native mobile application while also providing access to device features. Thanks to Adobe and the open source community, this technology has seen great growth over the years and more and more apps are being built with Cordova. The apps built with Cordova are commonly referred to as **hybrid applications**. But what is a hybrid app?

A hybrid application in the context of Cordova is actually a web app that lives within the thin container of a native mobile application.

In reality, the only difference between a native mobile app and a web application in terms of what they can do is the fact that the native mobile app has access to the device hardware features.

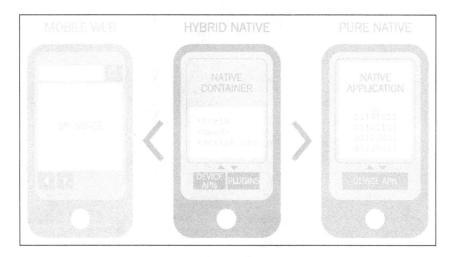

In truth, a hybrid app is actually a native app that serves up a web application on the phone's web view. It behaves and acts like a normal application and has complete device access, thanks to Cordova.

However, the main advantage that Cordova has over native development techniques is that you only have to maintain one code base, and can use that same code base to build applications for multiple platforms. This was and still is the main selling point of Cordova to date, as with this technique you are provided with a big cost and time saving advantage.

Early hybrid apps

When the first few hybrid apps started rolling out, there were a couple of problems that seemed to persist. The first problem was that a lot of people complained that these hybrid applications did not have the same user interface and user experience as native mobile apps. The major reason for this was that when building a native app, all the building blocks are already provided for you. For example, we have things like pre-provided animations, swipe gestures, tabs, and so on. Hybrid apps failed to provide similar features like these because on the web, all we have is HTML, CSS, and JS. There is no pre-provided component for things like animations, gestures, and tabs.

This meant that pretty much anyone trying to build a hybrid app had to build these features from scratch. This was not very good and different people had different implementations of the same features. As a result, a lot of applications that were built by the hybrid way were not so visually appealing. What we needed was a framework that was centrally maintained that provided us with all the tools we needed to build features that native apps had with web technologies.

What is Ionic?

Ionic is a framework that lets you build hybrid mobile applications with web technologies like HTML5, CSS, and JavaScript. But that is not where it stops with Ionic. Ionic provides you with components that you can use to build native-like features for your mobile applications. Think of Ionic as the SDK for making your Hybrid mobile application. Most of the features you have on a native app such as modals, gestures, popups, and many more, are all provided to you by Ionic and can be easily extended for new features or customized to suit your needs.

Ionic itself does not grant you the ability to communicate with device features like GPS and camera; instead, it works side-by-side with Cordova to achieve this. Another great feature of Ionic is how loosely coupled all its components are. You can decide to use only some of Ionic on an already existing hybrid application if you wish to do so.

The Ionic framework is built with AngularJS, which is arguably the most well-tested and widely-used JavaScript framework out there. This feature is particularly powerful as it gives you all the goodness of Angular as part of any Ionic app you develop. In the past, architecting hybrid applications proved to be difficult, but with Angular, we can create our mobile applications using the **Single Page Application (SPA)** technique. Angular also makes it really easy to organize your application for the development and working across teams while providing you the possibility of easily adding custom features or libraries.

Short history of Ionic

Before we dive in, first let's revisit what we already know about hybrid applications and how they work. Remember that a hybrid mobile application is simply a web application that runs in a web view, within a thin native wrapper environment.

Also remember that native apps came with already built components that enabled you to create beautiful user interfaces for mobile applications. Since hybrid apps used web technologies, there was no SDK or components provided for creating mobile UIs. The Ionic team saw this problem and created a solution in the form of the Ionic framework. The Ionic framework provides UI components to build beautiful hybrid applications.

Features of Ionic

Ionic provides you with a lot of cool neat features and tricks that help you create beautiful and well functioning hybrid apps in no time. The features of Ionic come under three categories:

- CSS features
- JavaScript features
- Ionic CLI

CSS features

To start off, Ionic comes stock with a great CSS library that provides you with some boilerplate styles. These Ionic CSS styles are generated with **SASS**, a CSS preprocessor for more advanced CSS style manipulation.

Some of the cool CSS features that come built-in with Ionic include:

- Buttons
- Cards
- Header and footers
- Lists
- Forms elements
- Grid system

All these features and more, are already provided for you and are easily customizable. They also have the same look and feel that native equivalents have so you will not have to do any editing to make them look like native components.

JavaScript features

The JavaScript features are at the very heart of the Ionic framework and essential for building Ionic apps. They also consist of other features that let you do things from under the hood like customize your application or even provide you with helper functions you can use to make developing your app more pleasant. A lot of these JavaScript features actually exist as HTML custom elements that make it easy to declaratively use these features.

Some of these features include:

- Modal
- Slide box

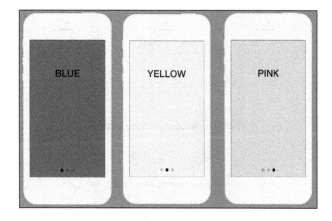

- Action sheet

- Side menu

- Tabs

- Complex lists

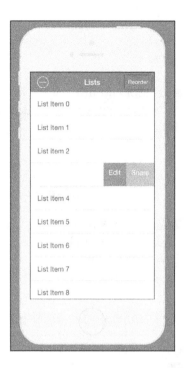

- Collection repeat

All the JavaScript features of Ionic are built with Angular, and most can be easily plugged in as Angular directives. Each of them also perform different actions that help you achieve specific functions and are all documented in the Ionic website.

The Ionic CLI

This is the final part that makes up the three major arms of the Ionic framework. The Ionic CLI is a very important tool that lets you use the Ionic commands via the command line/terminal. It is also with the Ionic CLI that we get access to some Ionic features that make our app development process more streamlined. It is arguably the most important part of Ionic and it is also the feature you will use to do most actions.

Ionic CLI features let you do the following:

- Create Ionic projects
- Issue Cordova commands
- Development and testing
- Ionic splash/Icon generator

- Ionic labs
- SASS
- Upload app to Ionic view
- Access `Ionic.IO` tools

The Ionic CLI is a very powerful tool and most of the time, it is the tool we will be using throughout this book to perform specific actions. This is why the first thing we are going to do is set up the Ionic CLI.

Setting up Ionic

The following steps will give a brief of how to setup Ionic:

1. **Install NodeJS**: To set up Ionic, the first thing you will need to do is to install NodeJS on your computer so you can have access to **Node Package Manager (NPM)**. If you already have node installed on your computer, you can skip this step and go to step 2. To install NodeJS on your computer, perform the following steps:

    1. Go to `www.nodejs.org` and click on the latest stable version for your computer. That should download the latest version of NodeJS on your computer. Don't worry if you are on Mac, PC, or Linux, the correct one for your operating system will be automatically downloaded.

    2. After the download is finished, install the downloaded software on your computer. You might need to restart your computer if you are running Windows.

    3. Open up the terminal if you are on Mac/Linux or the Windows command line if you are on a Windows machine. Type the command `node -v` and press *Enter*.

    You should see the version number of your current installation of NodeJS. If you do not see a version number, this might mean that you have not correctly installed NodeJS and should try running step 1 again.

2. **Install Ionic CLI**: The next step is to use NPM to install the Ionic CLI.

    1. Open a new terminal (OS X and Linux) or command-line (Windows) window and run the following command: `npm install ionic -g`. If you are on Linux/OS X, you might need to run `sudo npm install ionic -g`. This command will aim to install Ionic globally.

2. After this has finished running, run the command `ionic -v` on your terminal/command line and press *Enter*.

You should see a version number of your Ionic CLI. This means that you have Ionic installed correctly and are good to go. If you are on a Windows machine, you might need to restart your machine to see the version number appear.

If you did not see a version number, then you do not have Ionic installed correctly on your machine and should do step 2 again.

Summary

In this chapter, we started off by getting to know a bit of background about mobile applications in general. We learned how native mobile applications work, how they are built with native SDKs, and how each platform is built with a completely different set of tools without any resource sharing between them all. We then went ahead and discussed briefly about Apache Cordova and how it aimed to solve the problem of cross-platform development.

We then discussed exactly what Ionic means and what problems it aims to solve. We also got to discuss the CSS, JS, and Ionic CLI features of the Ionic framework lightly.

In the next chapter, we will be creating our very first Ionic application with the Ionic CLI, and we will create a nice to-do list style application with some great Ionic features.

2
To-Do List App

In this chapter, we will be diving headfirst into Ionic and will be using a lot of the Ionic CLI tool. We will create our first Ionic application and add some basic Ionic features to our app. We will also get to run our app for the first time using Ionic and will debug our app in Chrome. We will finish this chapter by creating a to-do list application with Ionic. This application will simply let us add items to our app and also provide us a way of deleting these items or marking them as done.

Creating our first application

Creating a new project with Ionic is actually a very pain-free experience with the Ionic CLI. There are different ways to create a new Ionic project but the easiest and more standard technique is to use the Ionic templates. This is by far the easiest way, and it let us use any of the three standard templates provided by Ionic.

These templates include:

- **The blank template**: This creates a new project with some boilerplate code to help you get set up with a blank application
- **The tabs template**: This is the same as the first but instead of a blank application, you get an application with a tabbed design
- **The side menu template**: This creates a new application with a side menu design and some boilerplate

We will be using each of these in this book at some point of time. For now, we are going to start with the first and create a brand new Ionic project using the blank template. Before we move on, let's have a look at the command that the Ionic CLI uses to create a new application:

```
ionic create [Name Of App] [template]
```

The `create` command for the Ionic CLI allows us to provide two parameters, the first being the name we want our app to be called. This first parameter will also be the name given to the folder that gets generated with our files. The second parameter is the template name. As discussed earlier, there are three template styles. You can either pass in blank, tabs, or side menu as a parameter to represent the type of template you want your app to be generated with.

Creating our to-do list app

We are going to create our to-do list application. We are going to use the blank template to do this. We will be calling our app `todo` for the sake of consistency. To create the `todo` app, go ahead and run the following command:

```
ionic start todo blank
```

This command will create a new blank Ionic application called `todo`. When this command has finished running, enter the project of your application via the command line by running the following command:

```
cd todo
```

To further explore our newly created `todo` app, open the `todo` app folder in your favorite IDE.

The Ionic workflow

When you create a new Ionic project, there are a couple of folders and files that come as stock as part of the generated project. Your directory should look similar to what is seen in the following screenshot:

The structure you see is pretty much the same as in every Cordova project, with the exception of a few files and folders. For example, there is a scss folder. This contains a file that lets us customize the look and feel of our application and will be covered in detail in later chapters. There are also the platforms and plugins folder. The platforms folder, in most cases is auto-generated, but we will not be covering them in this book so you can ignore them for the time being.

You will also notice that in your www/lib folder, there is a folder called ionic that contains all the required files to run Ionic. There are css, fonts, js, and scss folder.

- css: This folder contains all the default CSS that come with an Ionic app.
- fonts: Ionic comes with its own font and Icon library called **Ionicons**. This Ionicons library contains hundreds of icons, which are all available for use in your app.

- js: This contains all the code for the core Ionic library. Since Ionic is built with Angular, there is a version of Angular here with a bunch of other files that make up the Ionic framework.

- scss: This is the folder that contains SASS files that are used to build the beautiful Ionic framework CSS styles. Everything here can be overwritten easily in order to make your app feel a bit more customized and we will discuss how you can do this in *Chapter 7, Customizing the App*.

If you have a look at the root folder, you will see a lot of other files that are generated for you as part of the Ionic workflow. These files are not overly important now, but let's have a look at the more important ones in the following list:

- bower.json: This is the file that contains some of the dependencies acquired from the bower package manager. The browser dependencies are resolved in the lib folder as specified in the bowerrc file. This is a great place to specify other third-party dependencies that your project might need.

- config.xml: This is the standard config file that comes along with any Phonegap/Cordova project. This is where you request permissions for device features and also specify universal and platform-specific configurations for you app.

- gulpfile: Ionic uses the Gulp build tool, and this file contains some code that is provided by Ionic that enables you do some amazing things. We will use some features of this file in *Chapter 7, Customizing the App*, when we do some customization tasks.

- ionic.project: This is a file specific for Ionic services. It is the file used by the Ionic CLI and the ionic.IO services as a place to specify some of your Ionic-specific configuration. We will use some of the features of this file when we use the Ionic view app in *Chapter 3, Running Ionic Apps*.

- package.json: This is a file used by node to specify some node dependencies. When you create a project with the Ionic CLI, Ionic uses both the Node and Bower Package Manager to resolve some of your dependencies. If you require a node module when you are developing Ionic apps, you can specify these dependencies here.

These files are some of the more important files that are by default a part of a project created with the Ionic CLI. At the moment you do not need to worry too much about them, but it's always good to know that they exist and have an idea about what they actually represent.

In-depth look at our project

Before we go ahead and do any development, it is imperative that we understand how to actually add features to our app and where to do this. There are two files in particular that we are going to pay great attention to:

- `index.html`: This file is the entry point of your application in terms of what you actually see. It is a normal HTML page with some boilerplate code based on the blank Ionic template. If you pay close attention, you will see some custom HTML tags such as `<ion-pane>`, `<ion-header>`, and `<ion-content>`. These custom tags are actually Ionic components that have been built with Angular, and for now, you need not worry about what they do as we will be discussing this shortly. A closer look at the `<body>` tag will also reveal the attribute `ng-app=starter`. This is a custom attribute provided by Angular, which we use to provide the name of the main module of an angular application.

- `app.js`: This file lives in the `js` folder, and this is the file that contains the main module of our application. In Angular, modules provide us a way to create isolated chunks of code that our application uses. The main module is the module that actually gets loaded to our application when it starts. Think of the main module as the entry point of our application. If you take a closer look at the `app.js` file, you will see how we create the module and specify its name as starter:

```
angular.module('starter', ['ionic'])

.run(function($ionicPlatform) {
  $ionicPlatform.ready(function() {
    // Hide the accessory bar by default (remove this to
    show the accessory bar above the keyboard
    // for form inputs)
    if(window.cordova && window.cordova.plugins.Keyboard) {
      cordova.plugins.Keyboard
      .hideKeyboardAccessoryBar(true);
    }
    if(window.StatusBar) {
      StatusBar.styleDefault();
    }
  });
})
```

You will also see that it takes a second parameter, an array which contains
one string called ionic. In Angular, this array is used to provide the names
of any module that our application depends on. So, just like we specified the
name of our main module, starter to the ng-app attribute in the index.html
file, we specify a list of modules that our main module relies on, in this case,
ionic.

You would have also noticed a run function in the app.js. This function
is the function that fires as soon as our app is ready and all our dependent
Angular modules and factories have loaded. The run function is a great
place to do little pieces of tidying up that you want done as soon as your
application begins.

These two files are the ones you need to worry about as they are the two main files
we will be working with in order to build our to-do list application.

Envisioning our app

It is always good to do a small bit of wireframing before you build any application.
This enables you to understand how the app will work and how it will probably look
just before you actually begin to code the app. The following screenshot is a rough
wireframe of what our todo app will look like:

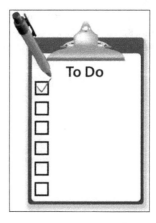

Our `todo` application allows a user to simply enter any task they want added to their to-do list. Think of this app as a mini diary where you put in things you want done later. In this section, we will only be building the very basic feature of our `todo` app, and we will only be allowing the user to add new items. In later chapters, as we learn more about Ionic, we will be adding more complex features like using a complex list and also letting the user edit, remove, and even archive to-do list items.

Building our todo app

To get started with building our `todo` app, we will need to further break down what we want to achieve into smaller steps. The first thing we need to do is to create the UI for our application.

Creating the UI

The first thing we are going to do to get started with building our `todo` application is building the user interface. We are going to build the input form and the button that will add the `todo` item currently typed in the input. After we have written the code for this, we will add the markup for the list where we want any entered `todo` item to be displayed. I have already compiled this markup for you in the following code:

```
<div class="list">
    <div class="item item-input-inset">
        <label class="item-input-wrapper">
            <input type="text" placeholder="enter todo item">
        </label>
        <button class="button button-small">
            Add
        </button>
    </div>
</div>
<ul class="list">
    <li class="item>

    </li>
</ul>
```

From the preceding code, you can see the skin of our user interface ready. We have an input that receives what we want entered into our to-do list. We have an HTML unordered list that will be placed where our to-do list items will be situated. You can see some classes on some of our elements. These are actually classes from the auto-generated Ionic CSS styles that come as part of any Ionic project.

The code

Since we have written the user interface for our application, we will also need to write the Angular code to enable it to work. What we need to do is to create an array that will hold the list of `todo` items and also create a function that will add a `todo` item into this list anytime we click the **Add** button we created earlier. We will achieve this all by creating an Angular controller in our main module and insert all this logic into it. I have already written this code and you can copy it and get it into your project from the following:

```
.controller('TodoController', function ($scope) {
  $scope.todos = [];
  $scope.todoModel = {};
  $scope.todoModel.todo = '';
  $scope.addTodo = function () {
    $scope.todos.push($scope.todoModel.todo);
    $scope.todoModel = {
        todo: ''
    };
  };
})
```

From the preceding code, you can see that we have created a controller called the `TodoController`. Within this `TodoController`, we have a `todos` array. This is the array that will hold all our `todo` items. We also have a `todoModel` object that is an empty object that will hold our entered `todo` item. Lastly, we have a function called `addTodo` that adds the current value in our `todoModel` object to our `todos` array and then sets the value of our current `todoModel` object to an empty string so we can type from scratch again.

Wiring things up

Now that we have created our user interface boilerplate code and also written our code for it, it is time to wire the two together and dictate what gets to appear where:

```
<ion-content ng-controller="TodoController">
    <div class="list">
        <div class="item item-input-inset">
            <label class="item-input-wrapper">
                <input type="text" placeholder="enter todo item"
                ng-model="todoModel.todo">
            </label>
            <button class="button button-small" ng-
            click="addTodo()">
                Add
```

```
            </button>
        </div>
    </div>
    <ul class="list">
        <li class="item" ng-repeat="todo in todos track by
        $index">
            {{todo}}
        </li>
    </ul>
</ion-content>
```

If you have a look at the preceding code, you will see that the UI code now looks a bit different. Firstly, we have associated our `<ion-content>` element with our `TodoController`. This is done in order to create a binding context, meaning any variable within the `TodoController` is now available for data binding to all its descendants. Secondly, you will also notice that our input now has a new `ng-model` attribute that binds to our `todoModel` variable from our `TodoController`. This is binding the value of the input tag at any point in time to the `todoModel` object. Thirdly, we have set an `ng-click` attribute on the **add todo** button to ensure that any time it is clicked, a new `todo` item is added to our array. Finally, we have done an `ng-repeat` within the UL element to specify that we want all children of the `todo` array to be rendered with the LI.

With this, we have successfully completed the `todo` application and all that is left is to see it in action. We will be learning how to run this application we have just built-in different ways in the next chapter, so do follow up to learn how to get your app to run and test it live.

Summary

In this chapter, we got to create our very first Ionic application using the Ionic blank application template. We had a look at what the Ionic workflow looks like and also got to see some of the files that make up the workflow. We then dived in and discussed about how we intended to build our to-do list application. We further went ahead and actually implemented the UI of our to-do list app based on a wireframe. We wrote some Angular code and wired it up to the user interface we created.

In the next chapter, we will learn different ways to run and test our application for the very first time with the Ionic CLI.

3
Running Ionic Apps

In this chapter, we are going to learn how to test and run our Ionic application using various methods. We will start by learning to test our application using the simplest Ionic technique: by serving our app to the Chrome browser using the `ionic serve` command. We will then go ahead and use the Ionic view mobile app for iOS/Android to see how we can test our application on a mobile device. Lastly, we will learn to run and deploy our Ionic application to a mobile device using the traditional build system of the native SDKs of our respective platforms.

Running our todo app

In the last chapter, we created our first Ionic application using the Ionic blank template. We worked on the application further, and made a to-do list app. We wrote some Angular code and had some initial exposure to some Ionic code. However, we did not get to see our application in action. There are many ways by which we can run an Ionic app, and the first technique we will be learning is the `ionic serve` technique.

The ionic serve technique

The `ionic serve` technique is the simplest way to see your app in action. It requires no extra setup after the Ionic CLI, and only requires you to have a web browser. We are now going to test our `todo` application, which we created in the preceding chapter using the `ionic serve` technique. To test your application with this technique, simply open a new command-line window and follow the following steps.

Browser choice

It is advisable that you use Google Chrome as your default browser. Google Chrome has some very powerful development tools and all exercises in this book expect that you have Google Chrome installed as your default browser. You can download a copy of Google Chrome by visiting this URL: `http://www.google.com/chrome`.

1. From your terminal, navigate to the root directory of your Ionic `todo` application.

2. Run the following command in your command-line window:

    ```
    ionic serve
    ```

In case you are prompted to select an IP address, you can select any one from the list prompted and press *Enter* to initiate.

If you followed the steps correctly, you should see a browser window come up with your app running in it. You will also notice that the command-line window where you typed the command has some things going on within it.

With this, we have successfully served our application to the browser and can test our Ionic application like any other web application on Chrome. The great thing about this technique is the fact that no extra setup is required, and all you need is just Ionic CLI and the Chrome browser installed on your machine.

Emulating with Chrome

Even though our application is served on the Chrome browser, it is fullscreen and is served like a normal fullscreen web app. This is not ideal for us, as our application is a mobile application. Luckily, Chrome has a neat emulation tool that lets you emulate your application as if it were running on a normal mobile phone.

To use Chrome's emulation feature, follow the following steps.

 These steps assume that you already have your app served on the Chrome browser and you are currently on the tab that it is served on.

1. Click the Chrome menu icon, as shown in the following screenshot:

2. Scroll down to the **More Tools** options and select the **Developer Tools** option, as shown in the following screenshot:

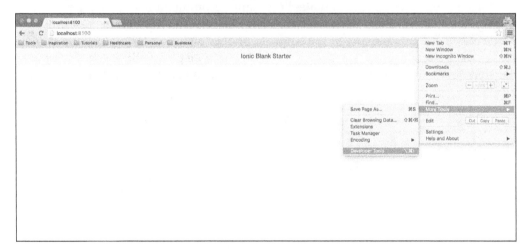

3. Click the **Device Mode** toggle icon, as shown in the following screenshot:

This should bring up the Chrome emulator window with your app running on it. You might need to refresh the page for it to render the app correctly. If you have a look at the window, you will see a dropdown menu on the upper-left corner that has a list of devices that you can emulate. I normally recommend using the Nexus 5 for testing Android and the iPhone 6 for iOS. The reason for this is that the resolution of the Nexus 5 eclipses many of the Android phones available today so using it as a basis makes a lot of sense. The same goes for the iPhone 6 as well; since it is Apple's flagship device at the time of writing, it makes sense to use it for emulation.

You can fully interact with your app as if it were running in an emulator. You also have the full power of the Chrome developer tools to inspect elements and see how the code of your application is represented. Why don't you have a go with your app and try and add some to-do list items and see them populating.

Ionic serve labs

There is another flavor in the `ionic serve` technique that lets us see our app the way it looks on both iOS and Android simultaneously. This technique is called the Ionic labs technique.

This technique should only be used to view your app and is not intended to be used for debugging.

To view your app using the Ionic labs technique, simply follow the following steps.

If you are already viewing your app using the `ionic serve` technique, simply press *Q* to quit the current session or close the command-line window and open a new one.

1. Make sure you are in the root folder of your project.

2. Enter the following command in your terminal:

```
ionic serve --lab
```

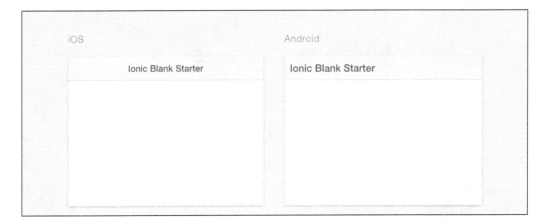

Running this should bring up a new browser window the same way as it did the first time when we ran the `ionic serve` command; only that this time, you will see two emulations for your app, one for iOS and one for Android, as shown in the preceding screenshot. This is a really nice way to see your app running in action on both platforms simultaneously. Ionic has a term called **Continuum** which you will see in action in later chapters. This phenomenon refers to the fact that certain elements look different on different platforms. For example, tabs on iOS are normally placed on the bottom, while on Android, they are traditionally positioned on the top. Ionic offers us these features out of the box with a further way to override these behaviors. The `ionic serve` technique is a great way to see the features like the tab positioned differently on different platforms simultaneously.

The Ionic view

Another technique to view an Ionic app is by using the Ionic view application. The Ionic view app is a mobile application created by Ionic with Ionic framework available on iOS and Android. The application is used to view any Ionic application you are developing and works hand-in-hand with the Ionic IO platform. The Ionic IO platform is a suite of tools that Ionic provides for some extra services like push notifications, analytics, and so on.

Testing todo app with the Ionic view

In order to use the Ionic view app, you must have an iOS or Android device. You must also possess an Ionic IO account. Navigate to `http://apps.ionic.io` to create your Ionic IO account. Go ahead and download the Ionic view app by visiting `http://view.ionic.io` on your mobile device and downloading the correct version for your mobile device.

In order to test our `todo` application, follow the following steps to test it with the Ionic view app:

1. Open a terminal window and navigate to the root folder of your `todo` application from `Chapter 2`.

2. Simply enter the following command on your terminal:

   `ionic upload`

This command will request the e-mail and password details of your Ionic IO account. Enter these details when prompted and if the app uploaded correctly, you should see a message saying `Successfully Uploaded (APP_ID)`, where `APP_ID` is an auto-generated identifier for you app.

Now you are ready to view the app on your mobile device. To do this, simply open your Ionic view app on your phone and login with the same Ionic IO account you uploaded your app to. You should see your application in a similar fashion to the following screenshot:

From here, you simply tap the todo app and a prompt will come up with a number of options. You should select the **download files** option. After this has finished, you can simply click the **View App** option. If you followed the instructions correctly, the todo app should replace your current view and you should see it running within the Ionic view app.

 You can simply tap the screen with three fingers to go back to the Ionic view menu at any time.

The Ionic view is a good way to view your application, and is extremely useful when you want to share progress with your friends, clients, or your boss about an app. It has a feature that lets you share to people's e-mails and you can find these documented in the Ionic official documentation. You can also manage the apps you upload to Ionic view from within the app or online via the Ionic IO website at http://apps.ionic.io.

Device

You can also test your Ionic application by running it on a physical device. To do this, however, you must have the native SDK for each platform installed on your computer. Let's take a brief look at how you can run an Ionic app on your device.

Android

To run an Ionic app on a physical device, first you simply ensure that you have your Android device plugged in via USB. You also need to ensure that you have developer mode enabled in your computer with USB debugging on.

 This step assumes that you have already set up the Android SDK on your computer and you also have Cordova and Ionic set up on your machine.

Ensure that you are in the root folder of your project in a terminal window and run the following command:

```
ionic run android
```

If you have everything set up correctly, this command will build your app and run it on the device plugged into the computer automatically.

iOS

To run an Ionic app on an iOS device, first you need to ensure that you have the iOS-deploy package installed.

 You can only deploy your app to an iOS device using a Mac computer. This step also assumes that you have the iOS SDK set up correctly alongside X-Code on your Mac computer.

If you do not have the iOS-deploy package installed, you can install it via NPM by running the following command:

```
npm install ios-deploy -g
```

Plug in your device to your Mac computer and ensure that it does not have the lock screen enabled. Simply run the following command to deploy your Ionic app to your device:

```
ionic run ios --device
```

This command should build and run your application automatically on your plugged iOS device.

Summary

In this chapter, we learned the various ways to test and deploy our app. We started off by using the ionic serve command to deploy our app to the browser using Chrome. We then had a look at how we can also serve our application using Ionic labs. We then went ahead to use the Ionic view application to see how we can run our app on an iOS and Android device with the Ionic view app installed in it. Lastly, we touched on how we can actually run our Ionic application on a real Android or iOS device.

In the next chapter, we are going to dive into some more complex Ionic controls, and we will get to use Angular's $http service to see how we can make Ajax calls and retrieve data within our Ionic application.

4
Ionic Components

In this chapter, we will be learning how to use some more complex Ionic components and controls. We will be creating a more advanced version of our to-do list application we created in *Chapter 2*, *To-Do List App*, using some more advanced built-in Ionic list components. We will call this more advanced to-do list application `Bucket-List` app. The idea behind this application is that it will allow us to enter all the interesting things we want to try in a lifetime. Therefore, we can enter the names of places we want to visit, the names of activities we want to do, and so on.

Creating a new to-do list application

In *Chapter 2*, *To-Do List App*, we created a simple to-do list application with the Ionic blank template. We were able to get this application to work by allowing us to add items into our to-do list application. We will be creating a new to-do list application using the Ionic blank template for us to add our new, more advanced components to our brand new BucketList application. Let's go ahead and create this new blank application by following the following steps. We will be calling our new application `Bucket-List` in order to differentiate it from the one we created in *Chapter 2*, *To-Do List App*.

1. To create the `Bucket-List` app, fire up a terminal window on your computer and navigate to the `Desktop` folder of your computer by running the following command:

   cd Desktop

2. After navigating to the `Desktop` folder of your computer, go ahead and run the following command to create the `Bucket-List` application based on the Ionic blank template:

   ionic start Bucket-List blank

3. This command will create a new blank Ionic application called `Bucket-List`. When this command has finished running, navigate to the project of your application via the command line by running the following command:

```
cd Bucket-List
```

Now you have successfully completed the process of creating your `Bucket-List` application, and we can start developing the app by adding features to it.

Overview of the Bucket-List app

To understand what we are trying to build, have a closer look at the following screenshot. We aim to achieve a final app that closely resembles what we have in the following screenshot:

Breaking down the app

A good way to build Ionic apps is by building them in bits. For our `Bucket-List` application, we can start by first developing the user interface and then writing the code behind it to enable it to work. Our user interface will contain an input box to enter a new item into our bucket list. Secondly, we have to design the UI for the list of `Bucket-List` items.

Designing the UI

Designing the UI involves two main implementations:

- Implementing the input box
- Implementing the `ion-list` element

We will have a look at each.

Implementing the input box

The first thing we are going to implement is an input box. This input box is the form where the users of our app will enter an interesting item they wish to add in the `Bucket-List` application. This will be in the form of an HTML textarea input box with some Ionic CSS styles applied to it in order to give it a more mobile look and feel. There also will be a button next to the input box with the label **ADD**. This button will be what we tap after we have typed some text and want it to appear as a part of our list. Perform the following steps:

1. Open up the `Bucket-List` application you created earlier in your favorite text editor.

2. Now, open the `index.html` file that can be found in the www folder of your project. You will see a screen that closely resembles what we have in the following screenshot:

```html
<!DOCTYPE html>
<html>
  <head>
    <meta charset="utf-8">
    <meta name="viewport" content="initial-scale=1, maximum-scale=1, user-scalable=no, width=device-width">
    <title></title>

    <link href="lib/ionic/css/ionic.css" rel="stylesheet">
    <link href="css/style.css" rel="stylesheet">

    <!-- IF using Sass (run gulp sass first), then uncomment below and remove the CSS includes above
    <link href="css/ionic.app.css" rel="stylesheet">
    -->

    <!-- ionic/angularjs js -->
    <script src="lib/ionic/js/ionic.bundle.js"></script>

    <!-- cordova script (this will be a 404 during development) -->
    <script src="cordova.js"></script>

    <!-- your app's js -->
    <script src="js/app.js"></script>
  </head>
  <body ng-app="starter">

    <ion-pane>
      <ion-header-bar class="bar-stable">
        <h1 class="title">Ionic Blank Starter</h1>
      </ion-header-bar>
      <ion-content>
      </ion-content>
    </ion-pane>
  </body>
</html>
```

You can see that this boilerplate code already contains some code for some custom Ionic elements just like we saw in our first application in *Chapter 2, To-Do List App* all of which are prefixed with ion. Pay close attention to the <ion-content> element! This element is the element that contains the bits and pieces of our application or the content area. It is in between this element that we are going to place all the markup for our Bucket-List application.

Let's start by placing the code for the input box of our application. I have provided the code for our input box in the following code block. You are to place this code within the <ion-content> element in your index.html file:

```html
<div class="list">

<div class="item item-input-inset">
<label class="item-input-wrapper">
<input type="text">
</label>
<button class="button button-small">
        Add
</button>
</div>

</div>
```

The preceding code is the HTML code that will display an input box and a button as we described earlier. If you pay close attention to the markup, you will see that some elements contain some classes. These classes are custom Ionic classes that are available as part of the Ionic CSS. The Ionic CSS comes with a lot of nifty classes and features, but for now just be aware of these classes and know that they are part of the Ionic CSS.

If you run your app in the browser using the ionic serve method, you should be able to see something that looks very similar to what I have in the following screenshot. Enter the following command in a terminal window to run your app using the ionic serve method. Make sure you run it from the root folder of your project:

```
ionic serve
```

You should be able to see the input box with the button placed on its right-hand side.

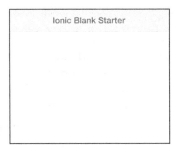

Ionic Blank Starter

Implementing the ion-list application

The next step of developing our Bucket-List application is to implement the ion-list application. We are going to use one of the built-in components called ion-list. The ion-list element is a component for creating and rendering lists. It has a lot of cool features that let us render complex lists that can have side options. Take a look at the following screenshot that shows the mail app from an iOS mobile device showing a list of features that we can implement using ion-list:

As seen above, one of the most obvious features we can implement with ion-list is the ability to show options when we swipe on a list item. It also has other features like the ability to delete items or rearrange them.

Using ion-list for our Bucket-List app

For our `Bucket-List` application, we will be aiming to use the `<ion-list>` component to render every item we enter through the input box. In addition, we would want to be able to delete each item from the list by simply swiping from the left and thus revealing a delete button, which we can click. The following screenshot gives a sample graphic breakdown of what we aim to achieve and what items are involved:

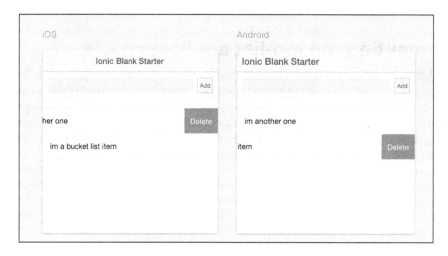

The ion-list component

The first thing we will do is implement the code for our `<ion-list>` component. The following code is the code for`<ion-list>`. You are to copy this code and place it just below the code for the input box you already implemented:

```
<ion-list>

</ion-list>
```

This is the top-level component needed to create our `<ion-list>`component. The `<ion-list>`component has some attributes that let us perform some more complex implementations. We will not be exploring these attributes but it is worth knowing that they do exist.

The next step is to implement the child item for our`<ion-list>` component. Each item in an `<ion-list>`component is called `<ion-item>`.

ion-item

As briefly noted in the previous subsection about the `<ion-list>`component, each item in an `<ion-list>` is called an `<ion-item>`. Within an `<ion-item>`, we will put the code for what we want each list item to render. It is also the `<ion-item>` where we will use Angular's `ng-repeat` feature. For our application, we simply want to render the name of each `Bucket-List` item. This means that we can think of every `Bucket-List` item as an `<ion-item>`.

For now, we are just going to have some dummy text in our implementation showing how a `Bucket-List` item will prospectively look. The following block of code is the implementation of our `<ion-item>` representing a `Bucket-List` item in our app:

```
<ion-item>
<h2>Bucket List Item</h2>
</ion-item>
```

This is a sample representation of our `<ion-item>`. If you still have your app running in the browser via the `ionic serve` technique, you should be able to see the `<ion-item>` rendered just like in the following screenshot:

Now, with that implementation completed, there is one more thing we need to do in order to finish the implementation of the user interface of our `Bucket-List` app. The one thing remaining is the delete feature. Remember from our initial implementation plan that we want the user to be able to swipe each item in our list and have a **Delete** button revealed. Luckily for us, the `<ion-item>` component has a neat feature for this called the `<ion-option>`.

ion-option-button

The `<ion-option-button>` component lives within an `<ion-item>` component as its child. Its sole purpose is to allow us to define buttons that we can reveal when the user of our app swipes from the right of each `<ion-item>`component just like in the original sample screenshot of our implementations. To get this implementation underway, copy the following code and paste it just before the closing tag of your `<ion-item>` component markup:

```
<ion-option-button class="button-assertive">
    Delete
</ion-option-button>
```

If you have a look at the preceding code, you can see that`<ion-option-button>` has a class attribute of `button-assertive`. This is also another Ionic class that is used to define a red button by default on Ionic buttons. Ionic has some built-in classes to easily add colors to elements. We will be discussing this later on in this book but for now just be aware of this feature.

By now, your final code for your`<ion-item>`component should look something similar to what I have in the following code block:

```
<ion-item>

<h2>Bucket List Item</h2>

<ion-option-button class="button-assertive">
        Delete
</ion-option-button>

</ion-item>
```

Your final code for your `<ion-content>` component should closely resemble what we have in the following code block:

```
<ion-content>
<div class="list">
<div class="item item-input-inset">
<label class="item-input-wrapper">
<input type="text">
</label>
<button class="button button-small">
            Add
</button>
</div>
```

```
</div>

<ion-list>
<ion-item>

<h2>Bucket List Item</h2>

<ion-option-button class="button-assertive">
            Delete
</ion-option-button>

</ion-item>
</ion-list>

</ion-content>
```

With this, we have completed the implementation of the user interface of our Bucket-List application using the <ion-list> component. Provided you still have your app running in the browser via the ionic serve technique, go and try to swipe the sample list item in your app from the left-hand side. You should be able to see a **Delete** button when you do this. See the following screenshot for guidance:

With this step completed, we are finished with the user interface of our application completely. Now, it is time we start to wire up the app by focusing on the Angular code that we will be writing to ensure our application works the way we want it to.

Writing the Angular code for our Bucket-List app

Before we begin, let's recap what behavior we want to implement in order for our application to work the way we want it to.

Coding our input box

The first thing we want is to be able to enter some text into our input box later. After we enter the text, we want to click the **Add** button and have this text entered into an array that holds all out `Bucket-List` items. To begin this first, we create our Angular controller that will hold all the logic for our app.

Creating the controller

Open to the `app.js` file of your application in your favorite IDE. This file can be found in the `js` folder, which is found in the www folder of your app.

```
www/js/app.js
```

There should already be a folder called `starter` with code similar to that which I have in the following code block:

```
angular.module('starter', ['ionic'])

.run(function($ionicPlatform) {
  $ionicPlatform.ready(function() {
    // Hide the accessory bar by default (remove this to show the
    accessory bar above the keyboard
    // for form inputs)
if(window.cordova&&window.cordova.plugins.Keyboard) {
cordova.plugins.Keyboard.hideKeyboardAccessoryBar(true);
    }
    if(window.StatusBar) {
StatusBar.styleDefault();
    }
  });
})
```

To begin, we will first start by creating a controller called `BucketListController` just after where we declared our module. If you have done this correctly, you should have code that closely resembles the following:

```
angular.module('starter', ['ionic'])

    .controller('BucketListController', function ($scope) {

    })

.run(function($ionicPlatform) {
    $ionicPlatform.ready(function() {
        // Hide the accessory bar by default (remove this to show
        the accessory bar above the keyboard
        // for form inputs)
if(window.cordova&&window.cordova.plugins.Keyboard) {
cordova.plugins.Keyboard.hideKeyboardAccessoryBar(true);
        }
        if(window.StatusBar) {
StatusBar.styleDefault();
        }
    });
})
```

With this done, we have now completed the process of creating our controller called `BucketLisController`. This controller is where all the logic for our app will live.

Creating the input box model

We are going to need to create a model that will be bound to our input box. This model will be in the form of an object, and it will hold the data that will be represented by the text we enter in our input box. We will call this model `bucketListItem`. To create this model, simply enter the following code within `BucketListController` that you just created in the previous step:

```
$scope.bucketListItem = {
title : ''
};
```

The preceding code is initializing the model for our `bucketListItem` model. This model has a property called `title` that will hold the text of what we type in the input box at every point in time.

Creating an array for the Bucket-List items

The aim of our app is to have a list of the `Bucket-List` items. These items, as we enter them in our input box, will need to be stored in an array. We are going to create this array, and we will simply call it `bucketListItems`. This array is what we will use in Angular's `ng-repeat` attribute to iterate and render in our view. To create this array for our `Bucket-List` items, simply attach an array called `bucketListItems` to the `$scope` variable of your controller. The following code illustrates this step:

```
$scope.bucketListItems = [];
```

Implementing code for the Add button

The final step to ensure that we are able to add items to our Bucket-List app with the input is by writing the code in the form of a function for the **Add** button. This button is responsible for two things. Firstly, it will ensure that the current text in our input box is added as an entry to the output box array of the `Bucket-List` items. Secondly, it will also clear up the model to ensure that after we click the button, the input box is cleared up for the next item.

The following code represents the implementation for our **Add** button:

```
$scope.addBucketListItem = function () {
    //Add Current Bucket List Item To The Front Of Our Bucket List
    Items Array
    $scope.bucketListItems.unshift($scope.bucketListItem);
    //Clear Current Bucket List For Next Entry
    $scope.bucketListItem = {
        title: ''
    };
};
```

From the preceding code you can see that we have created a function called `addBucketListItem`, and attached it to the `$scope` variable of our controller so it is available to our view. Within our function, we first add the current value of the `bucketListItem` variable to our `bucketListItems` array. Secondly, we clear up the `bucketListItem` variable to ensure it is cleared for the next entry.

Now, you can go ahead and implement the preceding code within your controller.

Implementing the Delete button

The last piece of our code is to implement the **Delete** button of our <ion-option-button>. Remember that we want this button to be able to delete the item which it belongs to. The following code shows the implementation of the **Delete** button:

```
$scope.deleteBucketListItem = function (index) {
$scope.bucketListItems.splice(index, 1);
};
```

The preceding code simply shows how we have created a function called deleteBucketListItem. This function takes in the index of the current item to be deleted as a parameter. It then uses this index to remove the corresponding element that is placed in that index from the bucketListItems array, which holds all our Bucket-List items.

With that complete, we have pretty much finished the code aspect of our application. Your final controller should look similar to what I have in the following code block:

```
controller('BucketListController', function ($scope) {
    $scope.bucketListItem = {
      title : ''
    };

    $scope.bucketListItems = [];

    $scope.addBucketListItem = function () {
      //Add Current Bucket List Item To The Front Of Our Bucket
      List Items Array
      $scope.bucketListItems.unshift($scope.bucketListItem);
      //Clear Current Bucket List For Next Entry
      $scope.bucketListItem = {
        title: ''
      };
    };

    $scope.deleteBucketListItem = function (index) {
      $scope.bucketListItems.splice(index, 1);
    };

})
```

Now, before we go ahead and test your application, we have one last step to complete. We need to wire up all the code we have just created with the UI we implemented earlier so that they can work together.

Wire it all up

With our controller ready, now we have to go ahead and wire all the code to the UI so that they can work together in harmony.

Binding the controller

The first thing we need to do is to wire up the controller we created. The simple and easiest way to do this is by simply using Angular's `ng-controller` attribute directive to specify our controller. In our case, we will be wiring the controller on `<ion-content>` of our app. Once again, open up the `index.html` file of your application. Find the opening `<ion-content>` tag of the page and specify an `ng-controller` attribute with the name of your controller.

Your code should closely resemble the following code:

```
<ion-content ng-controller="BucketListController">
```

This code is simply telling Angular that we wish to use `BucketListController` within the scope of this `<ion-content>` element. This means that all the methods and properties scoped within this controller are now available to the `<ion-content>` element and all its descendant elements.

Binding the input box model

The next step is to ensure that the `bucketListItem` variable we created in our controller is data bound to our input box in the view. Angular also has a simple but great attribute directive for this called `ng-model`. We simply provide `ng-model` with a value that matches an object or variable that we want to data bind to. In our case, we want to data bind to the title property of our `bucketListItem` variable from our controller. Again, I have provided the following code for your convenience:

```
<input type="text" ng-model="bucketListItem.title">
```

The preceding piece of code we just added tells Angular to bind this variable to this input box. Therefore, anytime the value of the input changes from the view, we have the same value in our controller and vice versa.

Wiring up the Add button

The **Add** button is next in line for our implementation. For this button, we simply need to tell it to run our `addBucketListItem` function every time it is clicked. Once again, Angular has a helper directive for this called the `ng-click` directive. The `ng-click` directive is like the classic Java `onClick` event listener and you provide it with a function that you want to run every time the wired element is clicked. The following code demonstrates how we can wire up our **Add** button with the `ng-click` directive:

```
<button class="button button-small" ng-
click="addBucketListItem()">
    Add
</button>
```

The preceding code implementation simply ensures that when the **Add** button is clicked, the addBucketListener function will run with its expected behavior.

Binding ion-item

The last part of our wiring up will be to wire our bucketListItems array to our Ion-Item elements, and also bind the ion-option-button element to our deleteBucketListItem() function.

Using ng-repeat to render the list

Right now we have a sample implementation that has one hardcoded ion-item. However, we will want a more dynamic solution where we automatically render the items within the bucketListItems array each as an ion-item. For this implementation, we are going to use one of the most important Angular features in the form of ng-repeat. The ng-repeat angular directive lets us dynamically repeat an array.

Right now, you have a code that looks similar to the following:

```
<ion-item>

<h2>Bucket List Item</h2>

<ion-option-button class="button-assertive">
        Delete
</ion-option-button>

</ion-item>
```

We are going to change this implementation to use the ng-repeat directive of Angular. The following code shows you how this is achieved:

```
<ion-item ng-repeat="item in bucketListItems">

<h2>{{item.title}}</h2>

<ion-option-button class="button-assertive">
        Delete
</ion-option-button>

</ion-item>
```

The preceding code now uses Angular's ng-repeat attribute. This code tells Angular to repeat the bucketListItems array and also binds the title of each item to an HTML <h2> element.

Wiring up the ion-option-button element

The ion-option-button element is still untouched and will do nothing if we don't tell it to do so. All we need to do for this element is to provide it with a function we want to be executed when it is clicked, like we did with the **Add** button. For this, we will be using the ng-click directive again, but this time, we will point it to the deleteBucketListItem() function from our controller. The following code shows just how we can achieve that:

```
<ion-option-button class="button-assertive" ng-
click="deleteBucketListItem($index)">
    Delete
</ion-option-button>
```

From the preceding code, you will notice one alien thing, $index being specifically passed as a parameter for our deleteBucketListItem function. This variable is a magic variable that the ng-repeat directive of Angular exposes to us. It represents the index of the current element being rendered by ng-repeat. With this index, we can learn what particular element should be deleted from our array of bucket list items, and delete the correct one.

The final <ion-content> in your index.html file should closely resemble what I have in the following code block:

```
<ion-content ng-controller="BucketListController">

<div class="list">
<div class="item item-input-inset">
<label class="item-input-wrapper">
<input type="text" ng-model="bucketListItem.title">
</label>
<button class="button button-small" ng-
click="addBucketListItem()">
            Add
</button>
</div>
</div>

<ion-list>

<ion-item ng-repeat="item in bucketListItems">
```

```
<h2>{{item.title}}</h2>

<ion-option-button class="button-assertive" ng-
click="deleteBucketListItem($index)">
            Delete
</ion-option-button>

</ion-item>

</ion-list>

</ion-content>
```

Testing our Bucket-List app

We have completed the implementation of our application, and now it is time for us to see it in action. Ensure you have your app running in the browser via the `ionic serve` technique, and test it. Try entering some things into your `Bucket-List` app such as skydiving, jet-skiing, and so on. You should see that every time you enter an item and click **Add**, the item will appear in the list and the input box will clear up ready for your next input. Also, make sure you test the delete option by swiping an item from the left to reveal the **Delete** button, and clicking it to see the item disappear.

Summary

In this chapter, we focused on creating our `Bucket-List` application from scratch using the Ionic blank template. We also learned to use the `<ion-list>` component of Ionic and its child elements. We wrote some Angular code to wire everything up and got it running. The `<ion-list>`component is a very powerful component, and although the task of this chapter might appear a bit more complex that the previous ones, there are still some more powerful features that the `<ion-list>` component lets us do. For more information about `<ion-list>`, visit the official documentation of `<ion-list>` from the provided links in the appendix of this book to learn even more complex features.

In the next chapter, we will be learning some very exciting stuff about creating side menu applications with Ionic. We will also build ourselves a tourist application and work with the AJAX calls for the very first time using Angular's `$HTTP` service.

5
The London Tourist App

In the previous chapter, we created an application called the Bucket-List application that enabled us to create a list of interesting things we wanted to do in our lifetime. In this chapter, we will create a new application called "The London Tourist" application. It is an application that will display a list of top tourist attractions in the city of London in England. We will build this application with a new type of Ionic template called the side menu template. We will also be using the Angular $http service to query our data via Ajax.

Introduction to the London Tourist App

London is the largest city in England and it is a city that is well known to attract tourists around the world. The city is very urban but it has many historical and non-historical tourist attractions. With this large number of attractions, it can be difficult to pick out the best places to go. This is the entire idea behind the London Tourist App as it will provide users with five handpicked destinations that tourists visiting London can actually visit. These destinations will be stored in a JSON file in our project that we will be querying via AJAX and populating.

Creating the London Tourist app

To begin the process of creating our app, we are going to start by creating a brand new Ionic application. So far in this book, we have learned to create a new Ionic application using the blank template. For the application we are about to build, we are going to use a new type of Ionic template to create the application. We are going to be using the side menu template to create our London Tourist app.

The side menu app design

You might not be familiar with what the side menu template looks like. In fact, the side menu design for mobile applications is very common in mobile app development. It involves having the ability to slide from the left or right edges of a mobile application to reveal more options, normally more menu options:

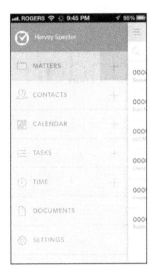

The side menu design technique is one that is used in a lot of contexts, both on mobile and on the web. Normally, you will see an icon positioned either on the far upper-right or upper-left, indicating that you can swipe or click that icon to reveal the extra menu options. This icon is normally referred to as the hamburger menu icon.

The Ionic framework actually comes built-in with a side menu template that automatically creates a side menu application for us with some useful boilerplate code. We will be using this template to create our London Tourist Application.

Using the Ionic side menu template

To begin developing our London Tourist Application, we will begin by using the Ionic CLI to create the app. You can do this by running the following command from a terminal window:

 We will shorten the name of our app from London Tourist App to LTA to make it easier to type.

```
ionic start LTA sidemenu
```

This command will create a new Ionic application called LTA using the default Ionic side menu template.

Seeing the LTA side menu app in action

As soon as your LTA app is created, you can simply change your directory into the app from the terminal and run it on your computer using the `ionic serve` technique. You can do this by running the following commands:

- Change directory to app:

  cd LTA

- Run using the `ionic serve` technique:

  ionic serve

 Remember to use Chrome and emulate to a device of your choice with the Chrome emulation tools as taught in previous chapters.

You should see a screen that looks something like the following screenshot:

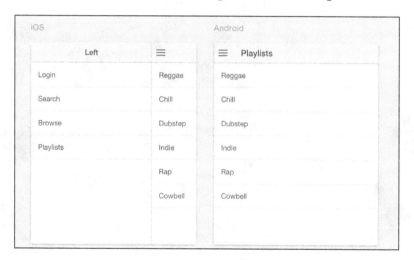

As you can see from the preceding screenshot, the side menu app we have just created contains some pre-rendered content.

Exploring the LTA side menu app's code

Now, we are going to have a look at the code of the LTA app based on the side menu template:

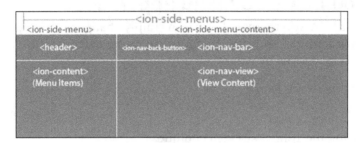

Now, I will require you to fire up the LTA project you have just created in your favorite IDE. The first thing you will notice is the folder structure that you are already used to from previous chapters.

The index.html file

Now, focus on the www folder and open the index.html file. A look through this file should show you something similar to what we have in the following screenshot:

```
<!DOCTYPE html>
<html>
  <head>
    <meta charset="utf-8">
    <meta name="viewport" content="initial-scale=1, maximum-scale=1, user-scalable=no, width=device-width">
    <title></title>

    <link href="lib/ionic/css/ionic.css" rel="stylesheet">
    <link href="css/style.css" rel="stylesheet">

    <!-- IF using Sass (run gulp sass first), then uncomment below and remove the CSS includes above
    <link href="css/ionic.app.css" rel="stylesheet">
    -->

    <!-- ionic/angularjs js -->
    <script src="lib/ionic/js/ionic.bundle.js"></script>

    <!-- cordova script (this will be a 404 during development) -->
    <script src="cordova.js"></script>

    <!-- your app's js -->
    <script src="js/app.js"></script>
    <script src="js/controllers.js"></script>
  </head>

  <body ng-app="starter">
    <ion-nav-view></ion-nav-view>
  </body>
</html>
```

 To get to this file from the root folder, navigate to www/index.html.

A look at this file will show you some things we have seen from previous projects in this book. For example, you can see some CSS and JS references to the Ionic `styles` and `script` files respectively. You will also see from the `body` tag that a generated Angular module called `starter` is being instantiated using the `ng-app` attribute.

Pay close attention to the `<ion-nav-view>` tags within the `<body>` tags. This is an Ionic element that is used to specify the view to which the entire app is injected into. It is similar to the `ng-view` feature of Angular but has more powerful features. It also automatically handles navigation for us within our Ionic app. You need not pay a great deal of attention to this part of the code anymore but just have it at the back of your mind that `<ion-nav-view>` is where all content gets injected in, and acts like a wrapper for our app's content.

The menu.html file

The next file we are going to explore is the `menu.html` file. This file is probably the most important file at this moment as it contains most of the generated code for the side menu parts of our app. To have a look at this file, navigate to the `menu.html` file which can be found by navigating into the folder called `templates` under the `www` folder. Here is the path: `www/templates/menu.html`.

If you have successfully done this, you should see a file that closely resembles what we have in the following screenshot:

The <ion-side-menus>element

The first thing you should pay attention to is the `<ion-side-menus>` element. Think of this element as a container for any side menu application. It allows us to specify what the main content area will be via the `<ion-side-menu-content>` element and also allows us to specify the side menus via the `<ion-side-menu>` elements. There can be more than one side menu specified within the `<ion-side-menus>` elements and we have the ability to specify whether the menu is placed on the left, right, or even both. There are a lot of cool and powerful controls that the `<ion-side-menus>` elements let us utilize to control its containing items. For now, we will focus on trying to learn more about the child elements that are needed to work with the `<ion-side-menus>` elements. These are the `<ion-side-menu-content>`and`<ion-side-menu>` elements.

The <ion-side-menu-content>element

This element is what houses the main content area or the visible part of the app:

In the preceding screenshot, which is a view of our LTA app, the part you see is a representative of`<ion-side-menu-content>`. Let's have a closer look at the code of `< ion-side-menu-content>` to see how it actually works in detail:

```
 2    <ion-side-menu-content>
 3      <ion-nav-bar class="bar-stable">
 4        <ion-nav-back-button>
 5        </ion-nav-back-button>
 6
 7        <ion-nav-buttons side="left">
 8          <button class="button button-icon button-clear ion-navicon" menu-toggle="left">
 9          </button>
10        </ion-nav-buttons>
11      </ion-nav-bar>
12      <ion-nav-view name="menuContent"></ion-nav-view>
13    </ion-side-menu-content>
```

Within `<ion-side-menu-content>`, you can see two direct child elements.

Firstly, you can see the `<ion-nav-bar>` element which is used to build the navigation buttons of the main content area with the`<ion-nav-buttons>` element as its child element. For example, within these`<ion-nav-buttons>` elements, you can see a navigation button on line 8-9, which has a `menu-toggle` attribute of value `left`. This is simply saying that when this button is tapped, the left-sided side menu should be triggered. Remember that there can be up to two side menus with one being on the left and one being on the right in a side menu app.

The second direct child element is the`<ion-nav-view>` element on line 12 from the preceding screenshot. We talked about this same element earlier when we had a look at the `index.html` file. This element is a placeholder for where the actual content is injected. This particular `<ion-nav-view>` element has a `name` attribute with the value of `menuContent`. This attribute is important as it is used like a value to uniquely identify`<ion-nav-view>`.

With all that said, we have now lightly touched on the `<ion-side-menu-content>` element and its main functions. Always think of this element as the element that houses the main content area of your side menu application.

The `<ion-side-menu>`element

The `<ion-side-menu>` element is an element that we use to specify the side menu of our app. Just like the `<ion-side-menu-content>` element, it lives as a direct child of the `<ion-side-menus>` element. There can be up to two`<ion-side-menu>` elements within the`<ion-side-menus>` element, with only one being on each side. Let's have a closer look at the code of`<ion-side-menu>` of our LTA application.

```
<ion-side-menu side="left">
  <ion-header-bar class="bar-stable">
    <h1 class="title">Left</h1>
  </ion-header-bar>
  <ion-content>
    <ion-list>
      <ion-item menu-close ng-click="login()">
        Login
      </ion-item>
      <ion-item menu-close href="#/app/search">
        Search
      </ion-item>
      <ion-item menu-close href="#/app/browse">
        Browse
      </ion-item>
      <ion-item menu-close href="#/app/playlists">
        Playlists
      </ion-item>
    </ion-list>
  </ion-content>
</ion-side-menu>
```

The preceding screenshot is from our `menu.html` file, and it showcases the code of `<ionic-side-menu>` from our LTA application. If you look at it closely, you will notice that opening tag of our `<ion-side-menu>` element has a `side` attribute with value `left`. This is basically saying that we want this particular side menu to be on the left-hand side. Remember that we can have up to two side menus in our app, and one can be positioned on the left and another on the right, but two side menus cannot be positioned on the same side. We can also see that this `<ion-side-menu>` has two direct child elements. These child elements are `<ion-header-bar>` and `<ion-content>`. `<ion-header-bar>` is an element used to construct the header of a side menu. If you have a look at the following screenshot of our side menu, you should see a representation of it:

From the preceding screenshot, you can see the header with the title LEFT as reflected in the code as an`<h1>` element.

The second child element we can see from the code is the `<ion-content>`element. Think of this element as what houses the content area below the header of the side menu. Basically, this is anything below the header. `<ion-content>` could contain any HTML code we want but in this case, it contains`<ion-list>` which is something that we used to build our Bucket-List application from *Chapter 4, Ionic Components*. You can also see a reflection of this code on the screenshot from when we ran our application.

With that said, you can see that we have successfully had a brief look at what the`<ion-side-menu>` element entails and how the side menu template of Ionic functions. The next step is for us to actually go ahead and build our LTA application in full scale now.

Developing the LTA application

We are now equipped with the know-how on how to code our LTA side menu based application. Remember that the idea behind our application is to have some of our favorite tourist destinations listed in our app. In a normal scenario, we would query this data from a real API. But for the sake of simplicity, we will mimic this API request by making a request to a local JSON file that would act like a real database with the information we need.

The local JSON database

As discussed earlier, we are going to create a JSON file that will act like a real-life API containing our destinations. This local file will contain five top tourist destinations in London. The first thing we will need to do is to create this file.

Creating the local JSON database file

If you do not have your LTA application open, make sure you open it in your favorite IDE. Now, go ahead and create a new JSON file called sites.json within the www folder of your project. Make sure you name the file as the .json extension in order for it to be parsed as a JSON file. Your directory structure should look similar to what is shown in the following screenshot:

With that done, you have successfully created your local JSON file representing your database for your tourist sites.

Populating the JSON file

Now we are going to populate the JSON file with some data. This data will be the data of five top tourist attractions in the city of London. The following is a JSON array that represents the content of our local JSON database. You should copy all the content of the following piece of code into your `sites.json` file:

```
[
  {
"id":"1",
"name":"London Eye",
"description":"Shows you a great view of the city"
  },
  {
"id":"2",
"name":"The Shard",
"description":"Highest building in London"
  },
  {
"id":"3",
"name":"Oxford Circus",
"description":"The place to shop in London"
  },
  {
"id":"4",
"name":"Buckingham Palace",
"description":"The Queen lives here"
  }
]
```

The preceding piece of code is a JSON array that represents four top destinations in London as JSON objects. Each object representing a site has three properties. These properties are:

- **ID**: A unique identifier for the site.
- **Name**: The name of the Tourist site.
- **Description**: Some small information about the site.

By now, we have successfully completed the creation of our JSON local database. The next step is to see how we can actually render these items and query the database.

Designing the view

We have created our app and we have the data for the application. Before we query data, we first need to design how the data will look when rendered. For this very task, we will call on an old friend of ours in the face of `<ion-list>`. We will use `<ion-list>` to render a list of tourist attractions from our JSON database.

Currently if we run our application, the first page we see is the playlist application, as shown in the following screenshot:

This is because by default the page is specified in the `app.js` file by Angular as the root page of our app. We will keep things simple and change the contents of this playlist page and design the view of our LTA application on it. From your LTA project folder, navigate into the `www` folder and look into the `templates` folder. Within the `templates` folder, there is a `playlists.html` file. This is the file that contains the code for our playlist page shown in the preceding screenshot. Open this file and you should see some code that closely resembles what we have in the following screenshot:

```
<ion-view view-title="Playlists">
  <ion-content>
    <ion-list>
      <ion-item ng-repeat="playlist in playlists" href="#/app/playlists/{{playlist.id}}">
        {{playlist.title}}
      </ion-item>
    </ion-list>
  </ion-content>
</ion-view>
```

> The `playlists.html` file from the root folder of your LTA project will have a path `www/templates/playlists.html`.

The first thing we will want to do here is to change the name of the title of our view. Currently, the view as seen from the screenshots previously, has a title `Playlists`. This is specified by the `view-title` attribute of the opening`<ion-view>` element. This `view-title` attribute currently has a value `Playlists`. Change this to `London Sites`. This is to ensure that the title reflects the mission of our app, which is to show the top London tourist sites.

The second thing we need to do is to edit the code for`<ion-list>`. Replace the `<ion-list>` code with the one provided in the following code block:

```
<ion-list>
<ion-item ng-repeat="site in sites">
        {{site.name}}
</ion-item>
</ion-list>
```

If you have done this correctly, your code should now closely resemble what we have in the following screenshot:

With this done, we have now completed the process of designing our UI. The next step is to go ahead and wire up our data to our view.

Wiring up the data

Earlier, we created a `sites.json` file that represented our database. We will be making a real Ajax call to this file in order to retrieve its data and serve it within our app. The thing we need to do to achieve this is firstly to write the code to retrieve the data.

Retrieving the data with the $http service

To retrieve the data, we will need to make an Ajax call to the `sites.json` file. For this, Angular has a great service called the `$http` service. This is a service that provides us with functionality to make Ajax calls to local and remote resources via Ajax. To begin using the `$http` service to write our code, we first need to go to the controller associated with our view. By default, when you create an Ionic app based on the side menu template, there is a controller attached to the views. To find out which controller is attached to our `playlist.html` file, we need to look at the `app.js` file of our app to discover this.

You can find the `app.js` file by navigating to the www folder of your project and looking into the `js` folder within it. You should see the `app.js` file. Open it. After you open this `app.js` file, look thorough the part where you have code that looks closely to what we have in the following screenshot:

```
.state('app.playlists', {
  url: '/playlists',
  views: {
    'menuContent': {
      templateUrl: 'templates/playlists.html',
      controller: 'PlaylistsCtrl'
    }
  }
})
```

The code from the preceding screenshot represents the state definition of the `playlist.html` file. Pay close attention to the part of the code from the preceding screenshot where the controller is defined and you will see that the controller specified there is called `PlaylistsCtrl`. This is the name of the Angular controller that our `playlist.html` file is wired with.

The next step is to go to this `PlaylistsCtrl` controller and write the code to retrieve our data. By default, the controllers are contained in the `controller.js` file that can be found in the same `js` folder as our `app.js` file.

Open the `controller.js` file and look for a stub of code that closely resembles what I have in the following screenshot:

```
.controller('PlaylistsCtrl', function($scope) {
    $scope.playlists = [
        { title: 'Reggae', id: 1 },
        { title: 'Chill', id: 2 },
        { title: 'Dubstep', id: 3 },
        { title: 'Indie', id: 4 },
        { title: 'Rap', id: 5 },
        { title: 'Cowbell', id: 6 }
    ];
})
```

The preceding code block represents the controller definition of `PlaylistsCtrl`. The first thing we need to do is to clear all the code within the controller. Basically, we need to delete all the code found within the controller. If you have done this correctly, your controller should now look similar to what we have in the following screenshot:

```
.controller('PlaylistsCtrl', function($scope) {

})
```

With that done, we can now begin to create the code to query our local JSON database with the angular `$http` service. The first thing we need to do to achieve this is to first add the dependency of our `$http` service to our controller. This step is very important as if we do not add this dependency correctly, our app will not load. To do this, simply add `$http` as the second parameter in the anonymous function part of your controller definition. If you have done this correctly, you should see something similar to what I have in the following screenshot:

```
44    .controller('PlaylistsCtrl', function($scope, $http) {
45
46    })
```

With that done, we can now go ahead and start writing the code to grab our data from our local database. To start this process, simply write the following code into your controller:

```
$scope.sites = [];
$http.get('/sites.json')
.then(function (response) {
    $scope.sites = response.data;
});
```

If you have done this correctly, your code should look very close to what we have in the following screenshot:

```
.controller('PlaylistsCtrl', function($scope, $http) {
    $scope.sites = [];
    $http.get('/sites.json')
        .then(function (response) {
            $scope.sites = response.data;
        });
})
```

At this point, I will explain what this block of code is doing. We start by simply initializing the variable `sites` as an array to the `$scope`. It is a good practice to always initialize your Angular `$scope` variables before using them. The next thing we try to do is make an Ajax `get` request using the shorthand `$http.get()` method. This `$http.get` method returns a promise so we handle this promise by using the `.then()` method of promise handling of Angular. In the promise handler function, you can see that we start by setting the data property of the response from the promise (`response.data`). This `data` property of the promise response (`response.data`) is the property that holds any data returned which in our case is the data from our `sites.json` file.

One thing that might be a bit confusing is the fact that, for the first parameter of the `$http.get()` function, which takes the URL of the API or the file we want to consume, we have provided the following relative path `'/sites.json'`. You might be wondering why we have not correctly given a path relative to the `controller.js` file. This is because when working with Angular, all paths are referenced from the root `index.html` file. In our case, the `sites.json` and `index.html` files are in the same directory under the `www` directory, which is why we do not have the path `'../sites.json'`, and instead have the path `'/sites.json'`.

With all this done, we have completed the process of creating our LTA application. All that is left now is to run the application. Go ahead and run this application using the `ionic serve` technique learned from *Chapter 1, First Look at Ionic*. Make sure you run this command from the root directory of your LTA app project.

If you have done this correctly, you should see a list of our tourist destinations as shown in the following screenshot:

Summary

In this chapter, we learned how to create an Ionic application based on the side menu template. We used this knowledge to create our London Tourist Application. We also had a look at the code that makes up an Ionic side menu template and learned about the building block elements of a side menu application. We rounded up by querying some data via Ajax using the Angular $http service and rendered our tourist destinations.

In the next chapter, we will extend our existing application and use some more complex Ionic components to do some really cool stuff.

6
Advanced Ionic Components

In this chapter, we will extend the application we created in *Chapter 5*, *The London Tourist App*. We are going to learn how to add some more complex features like the Ionic Popover and the Ionic Modal components to our current application. At the end of this chapter, we will have a popover menu and a modal window as part of our application.

The Ionic Popover

The Ionic Popover component allows us to add a popover menu to our application. A popover menu is a contextual menu that is used to provide a hidden menu or extra menu options. It is normally used when we have limited space and want to present a list of options. Instead of cramming our limited available space, we create some sort of button so that, when clicked, the popover menu can pop up and show these menu items.

The following screenshot shows a good description of what a popover does in reality:

Implementing the popover

We are going to implement our popover in our already existing application.
The first thing you should do is open your application, as you have left the London Tourist Application in the previous chapter. What we will be aiming to do is create a popover that has three extra options as a list. These three options are **About, Help** and **Logout**. These three options will not perform any action as we will only be placing them for the sake of example. The following screenshots show a sample of what we will be aiming to achieve.

- For iOS:

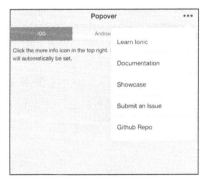

- For Android:

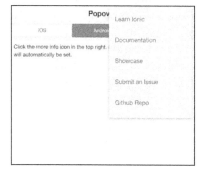

To begin implementing our popover, open the `playlists.html` file of your LTA application project. Remember that this `playlists.html` file can be found by navigating to the www folder and looking into the `templates` folder within it. Here is the path: www/templates/playlists.html.

Now, you should have a file that closely resembles the following code:

```
<ion-view view-title="London Sites">
  <ion-content>
    <ion-list>
      <ion-item ng-repeat="site in sites">
        {{site.name}}
      </ion-item>
    </ion-list>
  </ion-content>
</ion-view>
```

Adding the menu button

The first thing we are going to do is add the menu button that we want to trigger for our popover. This menu will display the popover when tapped. The following code block represents the code for button icon of our popover:

```
<ion-nav-buttons side="right">
    <button class="button button-clear icon ion-more"></button>
</ion-nav-buttons>
```

You are to replicate the preceding code just after the opening `<ion-view>` tag of your `playlists.html` page. The preceding code is using the `<ion-nav-buttons>` element to specify that we want to place a navigation button in our header. This element also has a `side` attribute with the value `right`. This `side` attribute is there to tell the `<ion-nav-buttons>` element which side of the page title to position itself. Within the `<ion-nav-buttons>` element is a simple button with some ionic styles that ensure that the button has an icon (`ion-more`) as our popover icon. If you have followed all the steps and replicated the code block correctly, your code should closely resemble the following code block:

```
<ion-view view-title="London Sites">

  <ion-nav-buttons side="right">
    <button class="button button-clear icon ion-more"></button>
  </ion-nav-buttons>

  <ion-content>
    <ion-list>
      <ion-item ng-repeat="site in sites">
        {{site.name}}
      </ion-item>
    </ion-list>
  </ion-content>
</ion-view>
```

At the moment, it is probably a good idea to test our application and see how our icon button looks. Fire up your application on a Chrome browser using the `Ionic serve` technique as we have done in the past. Your screen should look close to what we have in the following screenshot.

 If your title is centered to the left when using an Android emulator on Chrome, this is perfectly normal. The iOS equivalent will be centered.

Coding the popover

The next step is to write the actual logic for our popover menu. The first thing we need to do is go into our `controller.js` file. This file can be found by looking in the following path from the root of your project:

```
www/js/controller.js
```

Within the `controller.js` file, locate the `PlaylistsCtrl` controller. It is within this controller that we will be implementing our popover, as it is the controller associated with our `playlists.html`.

Adding the $ionicPopover service

In order to use the Ionic Popover, Ionic has a special service called `$ionicPopover` that makes this very easy. Add `$ionicPopover` as a dependency by specifying it as a parameter on your `PlaylistsCtrl` controller. If you have done this correctly, your `PlaylistsCtrl` controller should now look similar to the following code:

```
.controller('PlaylistsCtrl', function($scope, $http,
$ionicPopover) {
    $scope.sites = [];
    $http.get('/sites.json')
        .then(function (response) {
          $scope.sites = response.data;
        });
})
```

Finishing the popover code

The next step is to write the actual code to create the popover using the
$ionicPopover service, as shown in the following code:

```
$ionicPopover.fromTemplateUrl('templates/popover.html', {
      scope: $scope
    }).then(function(popover) {
      $scope.popover = popover;
    });

    $scope.openPopover = function($event) {
      $scope.popover.show($event);
    };
```

The preceding code block uses the $ionicPopover service to instantiate a new
popover. We also use the .fromTemplateUrl function of $ionicPopover to create
the popover. This function allows us to pass a URL for a file that contains the HTML
for our popover. The .fromTemplateUrl function also returns a promise which
returns the instance of a popover created. We then bind this popover instance to our
scope so that it is available for use in our view. There is, however, one small part
that we have not done. We passed in a file path templates/popover.html as the file
which contains the code for our popover. However, this popover.html file does not
currently exist so we need to create it.

Creating the popover.html file

To create our popover.html file, create a new file called popover.html under the
templates folder. This templates folder can be found under the www folder located in
the root directory of your project. Here is the path: www/templates/popover.html.

Now that we have created this file, the next step is to populate this file. Remember
that what we are trying to achieve is to have a list of menu items in popover.html.
We want these three options to be **About**, **Help**, and **Logout** to mimic a fake set of
popover options.

To start creating the content of our popover, replicate the following code block into
your popover.html:

```
<ion-popover-view>
    <ion-content>
        <div class="list">
        <b class="item" href="#">
            About
        </b>
        <b class="item" href="#">
```

```
            Help
        </b>
        <b class="item" href="#">
            Logout
        </b>
    </div>
    </ion-content>
</ion-popover-view>
```

If you have done this, you have completed implementing the template of your popover. Now, let's understand what the HTML code we just implemented on our popover.html file does. The <ion-popover-view> element is an element that is essential for indicating that this particular view is a popover. It also contains an <ion-content> element which is a container for all the visible parts of our view, or popover in this case. We then put a div tag with a class list which is one of the Ionic's built-in classes. Within this div, there are three HTML bold tags that represent our three fake options. That is all we need to complete the implementation for our template. The final step is to wire our popover to ensure it works as it should.

Wiring up the popover

This is the final step to get our popover to work. Remember that we created a function on our PlayListsCtrl controller called openPopover() which takes in a $event parameter. This function will initiate the popover when executed. We will also have to pass the $event parameter, which is a reserved parameter that represents an event sent from the view.

To put this into action, we will first need to wire this openPopover() function to be executed when the popover icon we created earlier is clicked. This popover button is in our playlists.html file from earlier steps. Your current playlists.html file should look close to what we have in the following code block:

```
<ion-view view-title="London Sites">

  <ion-nav-buttons side="right">
    <button class="button button-clear icon ion-more"></button>
  </ion-nav-buttons>

  <ion-content>
    <ion-list>
      <ion-item ng-repeat="site in sites">
        {{site.name}}
      </ion-item>
    </ion-list>
  </ion-content>
</ion-view>
```

What we need to do is add an Ionic tap event on the popover icon button that we created. We can do this with the Ionic provided attribute directive called `on-tap`. This `on-tap` attribute directive takes in a function which we want to be executed when the containing element is tapped. In our case, we want this function to be the `openPopover` function. Right now our popover Icon button code looks as follows:

```
<ion-nav-buttons side="right">
    <button class="button button-clear icon ion-more"></button>
</ion-nav-buttons>
```

Now, the code for the `on-tap` ionic attribute directive for `<button>` will look as follows:

```
on-tap="openPopover($event)"
```

You can see `$event` being passed as a parameter. Remember that this is very important and must be passed exactly as that. The final code for your `playlists.html` will look like the following code block:

```
<ion-view view-title="London Sites">

  <ion-nav-buttons side="right">
    <button class="button button-clear icon ion-more" on-
    tap="openPopover($event)"></button>
  </ion-nav-buttons>

  <ion-content>
    <ion-list>
      <ion-item ng-repeat="site in sites">
        {{site.name}}
      </ion-item>
    </ion-list>
  </ion-content>
</ion-view>
```

With that done, we have completely finished the implementation of our popover. Now, we can run it in our browser using the `ionic serve` technique to see what it looks like.

If you correctly ran your app using the `ionic serve` technique, you should see something that looks like the following screenshot when you click the popover icon button. The view will be different depending on whether you are testing with an Android or iOS emulator setting:

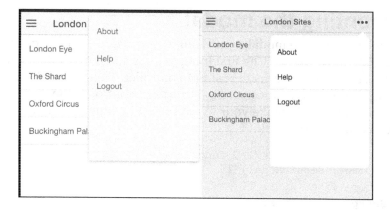

The popover is a great contextual menu tool for fitting extra menu options. It also has an automatic way of displaying a different version depending on what mobile operating system it is being displayed on. Now that we have learned how to use the Ionic Popover, let's learn to use the Ionic Modal.

The Ionic Modal

The Ionic Modal is a component feature that Ionic provides and is used to create a modal window in our application. A modal window is a view that pops up on an existing page without losing the context of your current action. As soon as it is dismissed, the previous view state is restored. It is a great tool for collecting extra information or displaying something on the screen without losing track of our current state.

Creating the modal

Ionic exposes the modal functionality via a service called the $ionicModal service. This service provides us a way of creating a modal in our application. Before we begin implementing our modal, let's understand what we aim to do with the modal feature in our application.

We will still be using our LTA application and adding a modal. We want this modal to mimic a sample **About** page of our application which will have some small details about the app. Remember that we already have a button from the popover we created earlier which has a text labeled as **About**. We will wire this popover item to simply open the modal when tapped.

Implementing the modal

To begin implementing the modal, open your `controller.js` file and locate the `PlaylistsCtrl` controller. The first thing to do is add a dependency to the `$ionicModal` service on the `PlaylistsCtrl` controller. This is done by adding `$ionicModal` as a parameter for the `PlaylistsCtrl` controller function definition. Doing this correctly should make your `PlaylistsCtrl` controller look like what we have in the following code block:

```
.controller('PlaylistsCtrl', function($scope, $http,
$ionicPopover, $ionicModal) {
    $scope.sites = [];
    $http.get('/sites.json')
        .then(function (response) {
            $scope.sites = response.data;
        });

    $ionicPopover.fromTemplateUrl('templates/popover.html', {
      scope: $scope
    }).then(function(popover) {
      $scope.popover = popover;
    });

    $scope.openPopover = function($event) {
      $scope.popover.show($event);
    };
})
```

The next thing we are going to do is write the code for our modal in our `PlaylistsCtrl` controller. The following code represents the code for our modal:

```
$ionicModal.fromTemplateUrl('templates/modal.html', {
        scope: $scope
    }).then(function(modal) {
        $scope.modal = modal;
    });
    $scope.openModal = function() {
        $scope.modal.show();
    };
    $scope.closeModal = function() {
        $scope.modal.hide();
    };
```

Replicate the preceding code into your `PlaylistsCtrl` controller. If you have done this correctly, your code block for the `PlaylistsCtrl` controller should look like the following:

```
.controller('PlaylistsCtrl', function($scope, $http,
$ionicPopover, $ionicModal) {
        $ionicModal.fromTemplateUrl('templates/modal.html', {
            scope: $scope
        }).then(function(modal) {
            $scope.modal = modal;
        });

        $scope.openModal = function() {
            $scope.modal.show();
        };

        $scope.closeModal = function() {
            $scope.modal.hide();
        };

        $scope.sites = [];
        $http.get('/sites.json')
            .then(function (response) {
                $scope.sites = response.data;
            });

        $ionicPopover.fromTemplateUrl('templates/popover.html', {
        scope: $scope
        }).then(function(popover) {
        $scope.popover = popover;
        });

        $scope.openPopover = function($event) {
        $scope.popover.show($event);
        };
    })
```

Now, let's understand what the code for the modal is doing. We used the `$ionicModal` service to create a modal via its `.fromTemplateUrl()` method. This method takes two parameters; the first being the path to an HTML file containing the modal, and the second being an `options` object. This `options` object lets us customize the modal and even provides us with ways to customize things like what animation to use. For now, we only specify the scope the modal should use, which in this case is the scope of our controller.

The .fromTemplateUrl method returns a promise with the created modal, which we set to our $scope. The following code is a reflection of the modal creation:

```
$ionicModal.fromTemplateUrl('templates/modal.html', {
        scope: $scope
    }).then(function(modal) {
        $scope.modal = modal;
    });
```

We also have two functions that we created. These functions are .openModal() and .closeModal(). The openModal() function is bound to the $scope, and all it does is use the created modal's .show() method. The .closeModal() function does the opposite by implementing the .hide() method of the created modal. One thing we have not done yet is create the HTML template we passed, which is the modal.html in this case.

Creating the modal.html file

Navigate to your templates folder and create a new HTML file called modal. html. The following code represents the template file for our modal, and you are to replicate this code into your modal.html file:

```
<ion-modal-view>
    <ion-header-bar class="bar bar-header bar-positive">
        <h1 class="title">About The App</h1>
        <button class="button button-clear button-primary" on-
        tap="closeModal()">Cancel</button>
    </ion-header-bar>

    <ion-content class="padding">
        The LTA app is part of the Ionic By Example book written
        by Sani Yusuf.
    </ion-content>
</ion-modal-view>
```

If you look at this code closely, you can see an <ion-modal-view> element as the root element of the code. This <ion-modal-view> element is the root element of any modal template. We can also see that we have an <ion-header-bar> element and this element has a <h1> element used to declare the title of the modal header. There is also a <button> element that has an on-tap attribute that is directed to a closeModal() function which we created earlier.

There is also an <ion-content> element which is used to contain the visible main body of the modal. There is some dummy text to mimic the **About** page of the LTA app, but feel free to add some of your own HTML text. The last step we need to do is wire our popover button to open our modal.

Wiring up the modal

To wire up our modal, remember that we want our **About** popover menu item to open the modal when tapped. To begin, first open the popover.html file of your project. What you have currently is as follows:

```
<ion-popover-view>
    <ion-content>
      <div class="list">
        <b class="item">
            About
        </b>
        <b class="item">
            Help
        </b>
        <b class="item">
            Logout
        </b>
      </div>
    </ion-content>
</ion-popover-view>
```

All we need to do is use the Ionic on-tap attribute on the About entry to reference the openModal() function. Doing this correctly will make our popover code look like the following:

```
<ion-popover-view>
    <ion-content>
        <div class="list">
        <b class="item" on-tap="openModal()">
            About
        </b>
        <b class="item">
            Help
        </b>
        <b class="item">
            Logout
        </b>
      </div>
    </ion-content>
</ion-popover-view>
```

With this done, we have completed the implementation of our modal window. The next thing to do is to go ahead and test this. To do this, run your application using the `Ionic serve` technique. When your app is up and running in the browser, tap the popover icon and the **About** option. This should bring up a modal window like the one shown in the following screenshot:

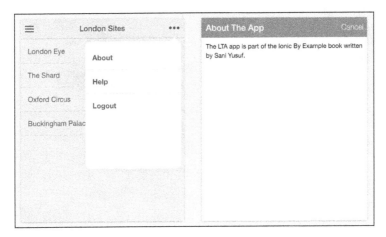

Summary

In this chapter, we used two very important features of Ionic and learned to create a popover and modal. We still used our LTA application from the previous chapter. The Ionic Popover is a great feature which is used to add extra menu items or provide contextual menu options. We also learned about the Ionic Modal, which is used to provide a view over another view of the app while maintaining the context.

In the next chapter, we will learn to use some of the customization techniques of Ionic, along with how to customize our Ionic app.

7
Customizing the App

In the previous chapter, we dug deeply into some more advanced features of Ionic like the popover and the modal features. In this chapter, we will be focusing on customizing an Ionic application. The Ionic SDK comes by default with some great tools that make it easy to customize your application to fit the design guides of your brand. This is thanks to its built-in integration of Gulp for your build process needs and SCSS for CSS preprocessing.

Ionic also has a special Angular provider called `$ionicConfigProvider`. This provider can be used to do a lot of configuration and customization like specifying what type of animations your application should use or even more advanced stuff like specifying how many cache items you want in your cache. The `$ionicConfigProvider` also lets you specify these configurations on a global level, or on a platform-by-platform basis.

Customizing the look and feel of your app

When you created an Ionic application using one of the Ionic templates, you would have noticed by now that it comes with some built-in default CSS styles. Many times you will want to know how you can add your own colors and styles while keeping some of the built-in Ionic styles.

Ionic styles with SASS

This is well thought out by the Ionic team and for this reason, they actually created all their CSS styles using SCSS. SCSS is an independent technology based on SASS that lets you write CSS in an object-oriented way which then gets compiled into CSS. SCSS is a really cool way to write CSS rules as it allows us to create variables and use them to create our style sheet. If you are completely new to SCSS and you want to see some brief information about SCSS, feel free to visit http://sass-lang.com.

Now, let's have a look at the folder structure of an Ionic project once more with customization of our styles with SCSS in mind.

Ionic SCSS overview

To have an overview of the SCSS structure of Ionic, we are going to create a brand new application using the Ionic blank template. We are going to call this application custom-app. The following is the command to create this new application. Fire up a terminal window on your computer and CD into a directory of your choice and run the following command:

```
ionic start custom-app blank
```

After you have created your new custom-app application, open this new project in your favorite IDE to have an overview of the folder structure. You should see something close to what we have in the following screenshot:

There are two folders that you should pay close attention to. The first folder is the scss folder found in the root directory of the project. This folder has a file called ionic.app.scss within it; we will take a look at this in more detail. The following is a screenshot of what this folder looks like:

The second folder is also titled scss, but this folder can be found by navigating to the following path from the root folder www/lib/ionic/scss.

The following screenshot shows this folder:

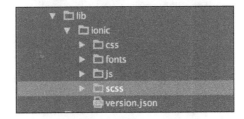

Now, if you look even further within this second scss folder, you should see something that closely resembles what we have in the following screenshot with a number of SCSS files within the scss folder:

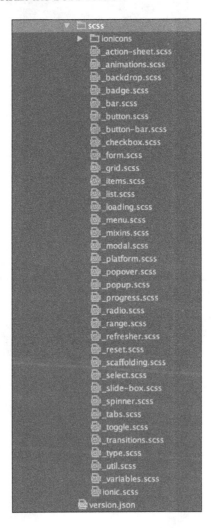

This `scss` folder contains a numerous amount of files and you might be wondering what these files are for. As a part of this book, you do not need to understand the entire process of what these files are doing, but you need to know that they are the files that contain the SCSS code for every Ionic element. The entire Ionic CSS style sheet is generated by compiling these SCSS files. It is possible to go into these files to make changes to any SCSS file, but this is probably not a good idea, as you will risk breaking any dependencies in the SCSS code. For this reason, Ionic provides a much simpler way to do this thanks to `ionic.app.scss` that we briefly looked at earlier and will be looking at closely now.

The ionic.app.scss file

The `ionic.app.scss` file can be found within a directory called `scss` in the project root directory, as shown in the following screenshot:

This file is the most important file for customizing the styles of your Ionic app. Think of this file as an interface for overriding any SCSS style contained in any of the SCSS files we noted in the `www/lib/ionic/scss` path. If you look at this `ionic.app.scss` file currently, it should look like what we have in the following code:

```
/*
To customize the look and feel of Ionic, you can override the
variables in ionic's _variables.scss file.

For example, you might change some of the default colors:

$light:                   #fff !default;
$stable:                  #f8f8f8 !default;
$positive:                #387ef5 !default;
$calm:                    #11c1f3 !default;
$balanced:                #33cd5f !default;
$energized:               #ffc900 !default;
$assertive:               #ef473a !default;
$royal:                   #886aea !default;
$dark:                    #444 !default;
*/

// The path for our ionicon's font files, relative to the built CSS in
www/css
```

```
$ionicons-font-path: "../lib/ionic/fonts" !default;


// Include all of Ionic
@import "www/lib/ionic/scss/ionic";
```

From the preceding code, you can even see some comments that tell you how to use the file to override your SCSS styles. Now, before we start learning how to actually override these files, first let's learn how to set up our SCSS for our project.

Setting up SCSS

Before we set up the SCSS, we will first have a brief look at how our CSS is currently integrated. When you create a new Ionic project, the project uses styles from two sources by default.

The first source is the `ionic.css` file which can be found in the path `lib/ionic/ css/ionic.css`. This file contains already compiled CSS code for all the Ionic default styles. It is simply a CSS compilation of all the SCSS files found in the `www/lib/ ionic/scss/ionic` directory relative to the root directory of your project.

The second source is the `style.css` file found in the `css/style.css` path relative to the root directory of your project. This file is normally empty at the time you create your project and is a place where you can enter your own custom styles in CSS, if you do not want to use SCSS. A look at the `index.html` file as shown in the following screenshot shows how these two files are referenced as CSS style sheets by default:

```html
<!DOCTYPE html>
<html>
  <head>
    <meta charset="utf-8">
    <meta name="viewport" content="initial-scale=1, maximum-scale=1, user-scalable=no, width=device-width">
    <title></title>

    <link href="lib/ionic/css/ionic.css" rel="stylesheet">
    <link href="css/style.css" rel="stylesheet">

    <!-- IF using Sass (run gulp sass first), then uncomment below and remove the CSS includes above
    <link href="css/ionic.app.css" rel="stylesheet">
    -->

    <!-- ionic/angularjs js -->
    <script src="lib/ionic/js/ionic.bundle.js"></script>

    <!-- cordova script (this will be a 404 during development) -->
    <script src="cordova.js"></script>

    <!-- your app's js -->
    <script src="js/app.js"></script>
  </head>
  <body ng-app="starter">

    <ion-pane>
      <ion-header-bar class="bar-stable">
        <h1 class="title">Ionic Blank Starter</h1>
      </ion-header-bar>
      <ion-content>
      </ion-content>
    </ion-pane>
  </body>
</html>
```

With this explained, we will go ahead and start setting up SCSS on our Ionic application.

Setting up SCSS can be quite challenging traditionally but Ionic comes built-in with some tools that make it easy. To begin the process of setting up the SCSS of your project, fire up a terminal window and simply navigate into your project's root directory by running the `cd custom-app` command.

The next step is to install `bower` on your computer if you do not already have this installed. You can do so by running the following command:

```
npm install bower -g
```

 You might need to prefix the `sudo` command if you are on a Linux or Mac computer. This will be `sudo npm install bower -g`.

After this, the final step to get SCSS setup is by running the following command:

```
ionic setup sass
```

This command will do all the necessary things behind the scenes that are needed to enable your project to work with SCSS. After this command is complete, you will notice a new folder called the `node-modules` folder in the root of your project. This is completely normal and is the folder that contains the packages necessary for your project to work with SCSS.

By now, we have successfully set up SCSS for our project. The first thing you should look at is your `index.html` file. Your `index.html` should resemble the following code block:

```html
<!DOCTYPE html>
<html>
  <head>
    <meta charset="utf-8">
    <meta name="viewport" content="initial-scale=1, maximum-
      scale=1, user-scalable=no, width=device-width">
    <title></title>


    <!-- compiled css output -->
    <link href="css/ionic.app.css" rel="stylesheet">

    <!-- ionic/angularjs js -->
    <script src="lib/ionic/js/ionic.bundle.js"></script>
```

```
        <!-- cordova script (this will be a 404 during development)
        -->
        <script src="cordova.js"></script>

        <!-- your app's js -->
        <script src="js/app.js"></script>
    </head>
    <body ng-app="starter">

        <ion-pane>
            <ion-header-bar class="bar-stable">
                <h1 class="title">Ionic Blank Starter</h1>
            </ion-header-bar>
            <ion-content>
            </ion-content>
        </ion-pane>
    </body>
</html>
```

The first thing you will notice in the header is that the reference to CSS files have changed in comparison to what we briefly discussed earlier. Now, you have only one CSS reference in the <head> part of index.html pointing to css/ionic.app.css. You might be wondering how this happened. Well, basically when you set up SCSS like we have done in this chapter so far, Ionic automatically sets up the SCSS to compile all the SCSS and output them into ionic.app.css.

If you navigate to the www/css path, you will see that we have three files as opposed to one as we saw earlier. You will see an ionic.app.css file and an ionic.app.min.css file. These two files are the same with ionic.app.min.css being a minified version of the ionic.app.css. They are the output of all the SCSS files that we checked out earlier compiled into one file. There are a lot more things that happen behind the scenes to ensure that this SCSS compilation happens, but for the sake of simplicity we won't be going deep into that in this book.

Customizing the SCSS

To begin customizing our app, the first thing you want to do is to run your application using the `ionic serve` technique learned from previous chapters in this book, using the following command:

ionic serve

This should bring up your application running in the browser and you should see something that closely resembles what we have in the following screenshot:

 Make sure you don't close your terminal or terminate the serve session from here on, in order to follow the instructions that come soon.

Now to explain what we will try to do, first let's have a look at the code for the head of this app. The code block is the code for our app and you can find this in the `index.html` file in the www folder of your project:

```
<!DOCTYPE html>
<html>
  <head>
    <meta charset="utf-8">
    <meta name="viewport" content="initial-scale=1, maximum-
      scale=1, user-scalable=no, width=device-width">
    <title></title>


    <!-- compiled css output -->
    <link href="css/ionic.app.css" rel="stylesheet">

    <!-- ionic/angularjs js -->
    <script src="lib/ionic/js/ionic.bundle.js"></script>
```

```
<!-- cordova script (this will be a 404 during development)
-->
<script src="cordova.js"></script>

<!-- your app's js -->
<script src="js/app.js"></script>
</head>
<body ng-app="starter">

<ion-pane>
  <ion-header-bar class="bar-stable">
    <h1 class="title">Ionic Blank Starter</h1>
  </ion-header-bar>
  <ion-content>
  </ion-content>
</ion-pane>
</body>
</html>
```

Pay close attention to the piece of code that represents the main view part of the preceding code block which is also represented in the following code block:

```
<ion-pane>
  <ion-header-bar class="bar-stable">
    <h1 class="title">Ionic Blank Starter</h1>
  </ion-header-bar>
  <ion-content>
  </ion-content>
</ion-pane>
```

If you look at the opening `<ion-header>` tag, you will see that it has a class called `bar-stable`. This is an in-built class that Ionic comes with which gives the header a sort of light gray color, as seen from the screenshot we visited earlier.

Let's say we want to customize this header to fit our brand color and let's say, for example, that our brand color and this brand happens to be my favorite accent of red which has the hex code of `#D71300`.

Now, you might be tempted to go into the `ionic.app.css` file to look for every occurrence of this in our CSS style sheet and change it. But remember that this `ionic.app.css` is generated based on our SCSS files. Ionic gives us a great way to override default styles with SCSS thanks to the `ionic.app.scss` file which can be found in the `scss` directory. We looked at this file earlier and we are going to look at it again:

```
/*
To customize the look and feel of Ionic, you can override the
variables in ionic's _variables.scss file.
```

For example, you might change some of the default colors:

```
$light:                    #fff !default;
$stable:                   #f8f8f8 !default;
$positive:                 #387ef5 !default;
$calm:                     #11c1f3 !default;
$balanced:                 #33cd5f !default;
$energized:                #ffc900 !default;
$assertive:                #ef473a !default;
$royal:                    #886aea !default;
$dark:                     #444 !default;
*/


// The path for our ionicons font files, relative to the built CSS
in www/css
$ionicons-font-path: "../lib/ionic/fonts" !default;


// Include all of Ionic
@import "www/lib/ionic/scss/ionic";
```

The preceding code block resembles what you currently have in your `ionic.app.scss` file. To override the color of the header, we will override the current color of the `$stable` variable of our SCSS.

The code for this is as follows:

```
$stable: #D71300;
```

You are supposed to replicate the preceding code anywhere but just before the last line of the following code block:

```
@import "www/lib/ionic/scss/ionic";
```

Now, your final code should resemble the following:

```
/*
To customize the look and feel of Ionic, you can override the
variables in ionic's _variables.scss file.

For example, you might change some of the default colors:

$light:                    #fff !default;
$stable:                   #f8f8f8 !default;
$positive:                 #387ef5 !default;
$calm:                     #11c1f3 !default;
$balanced:                 #33cd5f !default;
$energized:                #ffc900 !default;
```

```
$assertive:                         #ef473a !default;
$royal:                             #886aea !default;
$dark:                              #444 !default;
*/

$stable: #D71300;

// The path for our ionicons font files, relative to the built CSS
in www/css
$ionicons-font-path: "../lib/ionic/fonts" !default;

// Include all of Ionic
@import "www/lib/ionic/scss/ionic";
```

Once this is done, save the `ionic.app.scss` file. By doing this, you have completed the process of overriding the app, and your header should now be red. Go back to your application on the browser or run your app with the `ionic serve` technique if you don't have it running and you should see something that looks similar to what we have in the following screenshot:

You can see that header now takes the color of the hex code we provided in the `ionic.app.scss` file. We can override any default file with this file. All you need to do is have a glance through the `lib/ionic/scss` folder, identify the SCSS rule you want to override, and override in `ionic.app.scss`.

With this done, we have completed the process of learning how to override and set up SCSS of our Ionic app. The next step is to learn about `$ionicConfigProvider`.

$ionicConfigProvider

`$ionicConfigProvider` is a provider that Ionic exposes and which allows us to do some very powerful configurations. We will not be writing any code for this as it is an advanced feature but you should be well aware of its existence.

Some of the features that `$ionicConfigProvider` lets you do, include the following:

- Specify the transition type for your app
- Set the maximum cache
- Disable/enable animations
- Enable/enable native scrolling
- Specify tabs positions

These and many more are some of the features that `$ionicConfigProvider` lets you fiddle with. Remember that this feature is a fairly advanced feature and it is very likely possible to completely design your app without it. Most apps most likely do not use its features but if you find yourself ever needing to use it, you can visit the official documentation for `$ionicConfigProvider` to see its full potential at `http://ionicframework.com/docs/api/provider/$ionicConfigProvider/`.

Summary

In this chapter, we learned how to customize our application by setting up SCSS for our Ionic app. We also had a brief look at `$ionicConfigProvider` and saw some of its wonderful features. In the next chapter, we will get to learn how to create a new type of Ionic app based on the tabs template.

8
Building a Simple Social App

In this chapter, we are going to focus on learning how to create an Ionic application that has tabs using the Ionic tabs template. We will also have a look at some of the things that make up the tabs template and learn how to add features into it.

The Ionic tabs application

Tabs are a very common menu system in mobile apps. They provide users with a simple yet effective way to create independent views in an app that sort of act like apps within an app.

The preceding screenshot is a view of a sample Ionic tabs application. One great feature that a tabbed menu system provides is the ability to maintain the independent context within each individual tab menu. No matter where you are in the application, you always have the option of switching to another tab at any point. Navigation history is another feature that the tabs menu provides. You are able to navigate to different views within each tab, and you do not lose this navigation history when you switch back and forth between any tab menu. Now that we have some clarity about what the tabs application entails, let's go ahead and create a brand new tab application and look in detail at how it operates.

Creating an Ionic tabs application

Creating an Ionic tabs application is not too different from creating the side menu and blank Ionic applications as we have done in the previous chapters of this book. We are going to create a new Ionic tabs application, and we will call this application `tabs-app`. To create this new application, fire up a terminal window and run the following command:

```
ionic start tabs-app tabs
```

Using the preceding command, you will create your `tabs-app` ionic application successfully. The next thing we are going to do is to have an overview of the application we just created. To do this, simply open the `tabs-app` project in your favorite IDE. You should have a projects folder structure that looks similar to what I have in the following screenshot:

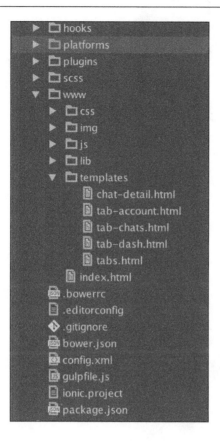

Running the tabs-app application

Now that we have created our app, let's go ahead and see it in action. To do this, fire up a terminal window on your computer and run your application using the `ionic serve` technique.

Make sure you are within your project's folder by running `cd tabs-app`. To run your app using the `ionic serve` technique, run the `ionic serve` command on your terminal.

You should see an application with three tabs that looks similar to what we have in the following screenshots.

- For iOS:

- For Android:

Overview of the tabs-app application

To begin to understand the life cycle of our `tabs-app` Ionic tabs application, we first need to have a look at the entry module of our application. Our entry module is normally specified within the `index.html` file of our app via the `ng-app` directive.

 The `index.html` file is located in the www directory of your application.

A look through your `index.html` will reveal a file that closely resembles what we have in the following screenshot:

```html
<!DOCTYPE html>
<html>
  <head>
    <meta charset="utf-8">
    <meta name="viewport" content="initial-scale=1, maximum-scale=1, user-scalable=no, width=device-width">
    <title></title>

    <link href="lib/ionic/css/ionic.css" rel="stylesheet">
    <link href="css/style.css" rel="stylesheet">

    <!-- IF using Sass (run gulp sass first), then uncomment below and remove the CSS includes above
    <link href="css/ionic.app.css" rel="stylesheet">
    -->

    <!-- ionic/angularjs js -->
    <script src="lib/ionic/js/ionic.bundle.js"></script>

    <!-- cordova script (this will be a 404 during development) -->
    <script src="cordova.js"></script>

    <!-- your app's js -->
    <script src="js/app.js"></script>
    <script src="js/controllers.js"></script>
    <script src="js/services.js"></script>
  </head>
  <body ng-app="starter">
    <!--
      The nav bar that will be updated as we navigate between views.
    -->
    <ion-nav-bar class="bar-stable">
      <ion-nav-back-button>
      </ion-nav-back-button>
    </ion-nav-bar>
    <!--
      The views will be rendered in the <ion-nav-view> directive below
      Templates are in the /templates folder (but you could also
      have templates inline in this html file if you'd like).
    -->
    <ion-nav-view></ion-nav-view>
  </body>
</html>
```

You will see an Angular module called `starter` specified as on the opening `<body>` tag of our page via the `ng-app` directive. This can be seen highlighted in the preceding screenshot. This `starter` module is normally located in our `app.js` file, and we are going to have a look at it to understand the module even more deeply.

 The `app.js` file is located in the `www/js` path of you project.

Open your `app.js` file and pay close attention to the `.config()` function where your routes are configured. Pay close attention to the first route definition of a route called `tab`. This route definition is represented in the following screenshot:

```
.config(function($stateProvider, $urlRouterProvider) {

  // Ionic uses AngularUI Router which uses the concept of states
  // Learn more here: https://github.com/angular-ui/ui-router
  // Set up the various states which the app can be in.
  // Each state's controller can be found in controllers.js
  $stateProvider

  // setup an abstract state for the tabs directive
    .state('tab', {
    url: '/tab',
    abstract: true,
    templateUrl: 'templates/tabs.html'
  })
```

This `tab` state is an abstract state. An **abstract state** in Angular is a state that you cannot directly navigate to but which can contain child states that can be navigated to. This is a great way to create some sort of hierarchy for your states.

Based on the state definition of the tabs as highlighted in the preceding screenshot, you can see that it references `templateUrl` to the `tabs.html` file contained in the `templates/template.html` directory. To understand how Ionic works with tabs, let's explore the `tabs.html` file.

Overview of the tabs.html file

When you open your `tabs.html` file, you will see something that closely resembles what I have in the following screenshot:

```
<ion-tabs class="tabs-icon-top tabs-color-active-positive">

    <!-- Dashboard Tab -->
    <ion-tab title="Status" icon-off="ion-ios-pulse" icon-on="ion-ios-pulse-strong" href="#/tab/dash">
      <ion-nav-view name="tab-dash"></ion-nav-view>
    </ion-tab>

    <!-- Chats Tab -->
    <ion-tab title="Chats" icon-off="ion-ios-chatboxes-outline" icon-on="ion-ios-chatboxes" href="#/tab/chats">
      <ion-nav-view name="tab-chats"></ion-nav-view>
    </ion-tab>

    <!-- Account Tab -->
    <ion-tab title="Account" icon-off="ion-ios-gear-outline" icon-on="ion-ios-gear" href="#/tab/account">
      <ion-nav-view name="tab-account"></ion-nav-view>
    </ion-tab>


</ion-tabs>
```

You will clearly see that the entire markup is wrapped within the `<ion-tabs>`
element. This `<ion-tabs>` element is the root element that acts like a container for
the tabs that you declare in your Ionic tabs application. You can see that the opening
`<ion-tabs>` tag also has a `class` attribute with some built-in Ionic CSS classes
provided. This is because the `<ion-tabs>` element is just like every other element
and is submissive to some CSS styling.

The <ion-tab> element

Within the `<ion-tabs>` element, you will see three distinct `<ion-tab>` elements.
The `<ion-tab>` element is the element used to create a tab and must be a child
element of the `<ion-tabs>` element. You will see that each `<ion-tab>` element has
some attributes. The `title` attribute is used to specify the title that that particular
tab will display. The `icon-on` and `icon-off` are attributes that are used to define
what icons get displayed when the tab is in focus and out of focus. Lastly, the `href`
attribute is used to provide the path of the route that should be navigated to when
that particular tab is selected.

 There are a lot more attributes that are available for different
customizations and actions for `<ion-tab>`, and these are all available
and duly documented on the official Ionic documentation page.

Within each `<ion-tab>` element, you will find an `<ion-nav-view>` declaration. The `<ion-nav-view>` is an element used to refer to an Angular view. If you pay close attention, you will see that the `<ion-nav-view>` elements have a `name` attribute, which has values. This `name` attribute is used to specify the name of a particular view that is defined in our `app.js` file. If you have another short look at the `app.js` file, as we did previously in this chapter, you will see that some of the states have views defined. A clear demonstration of this is shown in the following screenshot of the `tab.dash` state:

```
.state('tab.dash', {
  url: '/dash',
  views: {
    'tab-dash': {
      templateUrl: 'templates/tab-dash.html',
      controller: 'DashCtrl'
    }
  }
})
```

You can see that there is a `tab-dash` view named within the views object, and this `tab-dash` view has a `templateUrl` definition as well as a `controller` definition similar to a normal state definition. This is how Ionic provides a hierarchy that enables each tab to have a separate `<ion-nav-view>`, where its view is placed. To get an even better understanding of how this tab system works, we will be adding another tab to our application.

Adding tabs to the tabs-app application

We will add one new tab which will contain a feature that will let users post messages like a message board and see that it appears similar to a Facebook wall or a Twitter wall. We will be calling this new tab the `wall` tab. To add this new tab, the first thing we need to do is to add the route for our new tab.

Adding the state for the new tab

To add the state for our new tab, we need to define this tab in our `app.js` file where all our default tab routes are defined. Within the `.config()` function found in your `app.js` file, place the following block of code just after the state definition of the tab abstract state:

```
    .state('tab.wall', {
        url: '/wall',
        views: {
          'tab-wall': {
            templateUrl: 'templates/tab-wall.html',
            controller: 'WallController'
          }
        }
    })
```

If you have done this correctly, parts of the .config() function of your app.js file should look something like this:

```
.config(function($stateProvider, $urlRouterProvider) {

  $stateProvider

    // setup an abstract state for the tabs directive
    .state('tab', {
    url: '/tab',
    abstract: true,
    templateUrl: 'templates/tabs.html'
    })

    .state('tab.wall', {
    url: '/wall',
    views: {
      'tab-wall': {
        templateUrl: 'templates/tab-wall.html',
        controller: 'WallController'
      }
    }
    })
    // Each tab has its own nav history stack:

    .state('tab.dash', {
    url: '/dash',
    views: {
      'tab-dash': {
        templateUrl: 'templates/tab-dash.html',
        controller: 'DashCtrl'
      }
    }
    })
```

Let's try to understand what we have just done here. We have created a new state called tab.wall, which has a route /tab. This means that we are able to navigate to this tab.wall state or /tab route as part of our Angular application. We have also created a new view called tab-wall, and later in this chapter, we will use this tab-wall view to reference it as where we want the content of our newly created tab to be displayed.

If you take a closer look at our new state definition, you will see that we referenced a `templateUrl` to a file with the path `templates/tab-wall.html` and a controller, `WallController`, both of which we have not yet created. We will need to create this `tab-wall.html` file and also create the `WallController` controller.

Creating the tab-wall.html file

To create the `tab-wall.html` file correctly, we need to make sure that we create it within the `templates` directory in order for it to match the `templates/tab-wall.html` directory which we passed when declaring our state definition.

Create a file called `tab-wall.html` within your `templates` folder. If you have done this correctly, your `templates` directory should look something very similar to what we have in the following screenshot:

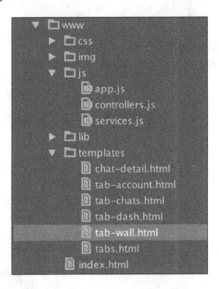

The next step is to actually populate the newly created `tab-wall.html` file. Place the code as shown in the following code block into your `tab-wall.html` file:

```
<ion-view view-title="Wall">
  <ion-content class="padding">

    <div class="list">
      <div class="item item-input-inset">
```

```
      <label class="item-input-wrapper">
        <input type="text" placeholder="enter your message">
      </label>
      <button class="button button-small">
        Post
      </button>
    </div>
  </div>

  <div class="card">
    <div class="item item-text-wrap">
      This Is A Sample Message Post
    </div>
  </div>

  </ion-content>
</ion-view>
```

If you have correctly done this, your `tab-wall.html` should look something like the following screenshot:

```
<ion-view view-title="Wall">
  <ion-content class="padding">

    <div class="list">
      <div class="item item-input-inset">
        <label class="item-input-wrapper">
          <input type="text" placeholder="enter your message">
        </label>
        <button class="button button-small">
          Post
        </button>
      </div>
    </div>

    <div class="card">
      <div class="item item-text-wrap">
        This Is A Sample Message Post
      </div>
    </div>

  </ion-content>
</ion-view>
```

This next step is to create the controller we defined in our state definition.

Creating the WallController controller

To create the `WallController` controller, first we need to open the `controller.js` file. This file can be found within the same folder as our `app.js` file, that is, the JS folder. Your `controller.js` file should closely resemble what we have in the following screenshot:

```
angular.module('starter.controllers', [])

.controller('DashCtrl', function($scope) {})

.controller('ChatsCtrl', function($scope, Chats) {
  // With the new view caching in Ionic, Controllers are only called
  // when they are recreated or on app start, instead of every page change.
  // To listen for when this page is active (for example, to refresh data),
  // listen for the $ionicView.enter event:
  //
  //$scope.$on('$ionicView.enter', function(e) {
  //});

  $scope.chats = Chats.all();
  $scope.remove = function(chat) {
    Chats.remove(chat);
  };
})

.controller('ChatDetailCtrl', function($scope, $stateParams, Chats) {
  $scope.chat = Chats.get($stateParams.chatId);
})

.controller('AccountCtrl', function($scope) {
  $scope.settings = {
    enableFriends: true
  };
});
```

To create the `WallController` file, simply place the code found in the following code block just after the first line where you can find the line of code, `angular.module('starter.controllers', [])`:

```
.controller('WallController', function($scope) {

})
```

If you have correctly replicated this code, your `controller.js` file should closely resemble to the following screenshot:

```
angular.module('starter.controllers', [])

.controller('WallController', function($scope) {

})

.controller('DashCtrl', function($scope) {})

.controller('ChatsCtrl', function($scope, Chats) {
  // With the new view caching in Ionic, Controllers are only called
  // when they are recreated or on app start, instead of every page change.
  // To listen for when this page is active (for example, to refresh data),
  // listen for the $ionicView.enter event:
  //
  //$scope.$on('$ionicView.enter', function(e) {
  //});

  $scope.chats = Chats.all();
  $scope.remove = function(chat) {
    Chats.remove(chat);
  };
})

.controller('ChatDetailCtrl', function($scope, $stateParams, Chats) {
  $scope.chat = Chats.get($stateParams.chatId);
})

.controller('AccountCtrl', function($scope) {
  $scope.settings = {
    enableFriends: true
  };
});
```

By doing this, we have successfully created the `WallController` controller. However, we still have one last step to complete the implementation of our new tab. We need to actually create the tab itself using the `<ion-tab>` element.

Creating the tab

To create our tab, we need to revisit the `tabs.html` file. Within the file, locate the opening `<ion-tabs>` tag and place the code mentioned in the following code block just after that:

```
<!-- Wall Tab -->
  <ion-tab title="Wall" icon-off="ion-ios-compose-outline" icon-
    on="ion-ios-compose" href="#/tab/wall">
    <ion-nav-view name="tab-wall"></ion-nav-view>
  </ion-tab>
```

If you have done this correctly, your `tabs.html` file should look like what is shown in the following screenshot:

By doing this, we have successfully created a new tab in our application. Let's recap what we did to achieve this feat. First, we created a new state definition for our tab and referenced it a controller and template file. We then went ahead to create the tab itself using the `<ion-tab>` element, as in the preceding screenshot.

If you look at the preceding screenshot and pay close attention to `<ion-tab>` that we just replicated from the code block, you will see that its `<ion-nav-view>` child element has a `name` attribute with the value `tab-wall`. This is simply referencing the view we defined while defining our `tab.wall` state in our `app.js` file. These steps complete our tabs implementation.

Now, the next step is to go on and run our app and see it in action. To do this, simply run your application using the `ionic serve` technique.

 To run your app using the `ionic serve` technique, simply run `ionic serve` from the root directory of your `tab-app` application.

If you have done this correctly, you should see something that closely resembles what we have in the following screenshots.

- For iOS:

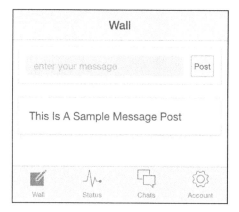

- For Android:

Summary

In this chapter, we learned about the Ionic tabs application template. We also created a tabs application called `tabs-app` and even got as far as adding a new tab of our own. In the next chapter, we will be using this same application to learn how to use Firebase to add backend services to our application.

9

Connecting to Firebase

In this chapter, we are going to focus solely on learning how to use Firebase to integrate a backend with our Ionic application. Firebase is a real-time data store technology that uses JSON-style database structure to let you store your data in the cloud. We will also be using the `tabs-app` app that we created in *Chapter 8, Building a Simple Social App,* to learn to integrate Firebase into our application.

Extending our tabs-app Ionic app

In *Chapter 8, Building a Simple Social App,* we created `tabs-app`. If you recall correctly, we added a new tab called `walls`.

The basic idea we had for the `wall` tab we added was that it would be like a message board where a user could type a post and then tap the button labeled **Post** to see it on the message board, as shown in the following screenshot:

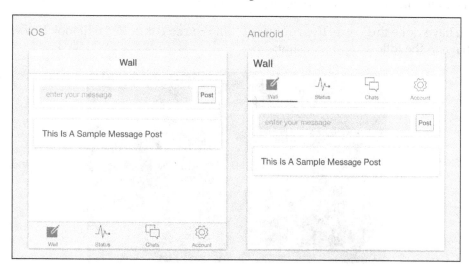

The first thing we need to do is to implement our mechanism to allow users to post, as this does not currently work in our `tab-app` application.

Implementing the post wall feature

To recap what we want from our `wall` tab, we want to be able to enter message in the message box, as seen in the preceding screenshot, and have the message appear like the sample message post. To begin, we start by implementing the code for adding a post in our controller.

This code is provided in the following code block:

```
$scope.post = {
    message : ''
};

$scope.posts = [];

$scope.addPost = function () {
  $scope.posts.unshift($scope.post);

  $scope.post = {
    message: ''
  };
};
```

You will need to replicate the code provided in the preceding block within your `WallController` controller. This `WallController` controller can be found within the `controller.js` file of your `tabs-app` application. The `WallController` controller can be found in the path `www/js/controller.js`.

If you have done this correctly, your `WallController` controller will look like what we have in the following screenshot:

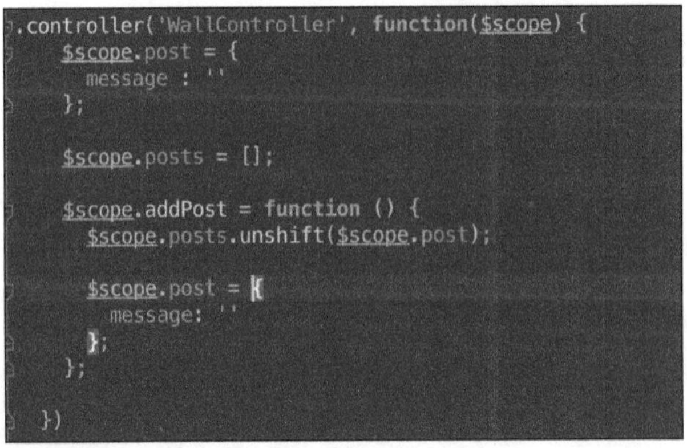

Let's understand what this code is doing. We are simply attaching a `post` object to the controller. We are also declaring a `posts` array where all our posts will be stored.

Lastly, we have a function called `addPost()` which will add a new post to the `posts` array every time it is fired.

The next step is to wire this controller into the view of our `Wall` tab. The markup for this view is located in the `tab-wall.html` file. Now, this file looks like what we have in the following screenshot:

```
<ion-view view-title="Wall">
  <ion-content class="padding">

    <div class="list">
      <div class="item item-input-inset">
        <label class="item-input-wrapper">
          <input type="text" placeholder="enter your message">
        </label>
        <button class="button button-small">
          Post
        </button>
      </div>
    </div>

    <div class="card">
      <div class="item item-text-wrap">
        This Is A Sample Message Post
      </div>
    </div>

  </ion-content>
</ion-view>
```

You will need to completely replace the markup found within `<ion-content>` with the markup provided in the following code block:

```
<div class="list">
    <div class="item item-input-inset">
      <label class="item-input-wrapper">
        <input type="text" placeholder="enter your message"
        ng-model="post.message">
      </label>
      <button class="button button-small" on-tap="addPost()">
        Post
      </button>
    </div>
  </div>

  <div class="card" ng-repeat="post in posts">
    <div class="item item-text-wrap">
```

```
      {{post.message}}
    </div>
  </div>
```

If you have done this correctly, your `tab-wall.html` file will have a markup that looks like the following screenshot:

```
<ion-view view-title="Wall">
  <ion-content class="padding">

    <div class="list">
      <div class="item item-input-inset">
        <label class="item-input-wrapper">
          <input type="text" placeholder="enter your message" ng-model="post.message">
        </label>
        <button class="button button-small" on-tap="addPost()">
          Post
        </button>
      </div>
    </div>

    <div class="card" ng-repeat="post in posts">
      <div class="item item-text-wrap">
        {{post.message}}
      </div>
    </div>

  </ion-content>
</ion-view>
```

By doing this, we have completed the process of implementing and wiring our wall post feature on the `Wall` tab. The next step is to test it using the `ionic serve` technique. Go ahead and run your app using the `ionic serve` technique and you should see your app running in the browser.

If you try to add a message in the text box found in the `Wall` tab and click the **Post** button, you will see a message appear, like what we have in the following screenshot:

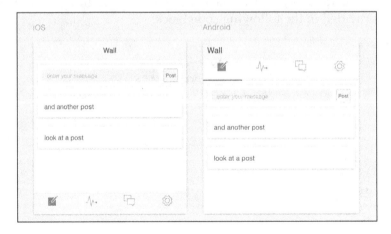

The backend challenge

The one problem or challenge we have with our current application is that it does not persist. By this, we mean that once we refresh the browser, all our data is gone and we have to start again. How cool would it be if we could enter a post and when we revisited our app, we could carry on from where we left off just like every other message board in other applications? Well, we can achieve this thanks to a great technology called Firebase. The first thing we will do is try to understand Firebase and what exactly it is.

Firebase

Before we begin this chapter, it is very important that we understand the technology we are going to be using to integrate our backend. The technology in question is called Firebase. Firebase is a technology that lets us store real-time data. Unlike traditional backend databases where you need a server running, you do not need to have a hosted server with Firebase.

All you need to get going with Firebase is an active Google account and you are good to go. Let's set up a new Firebase account.

If you do not have a Google account, you can create one by visiting `http://www.gmail.com`.

Setting up a new Firebase account

The first thing you need to do to set up your Firebase account is go to the Firebase website, which is `http://www.firebase.com`.

You should see a screen that looks like what we have in the following screenshot:

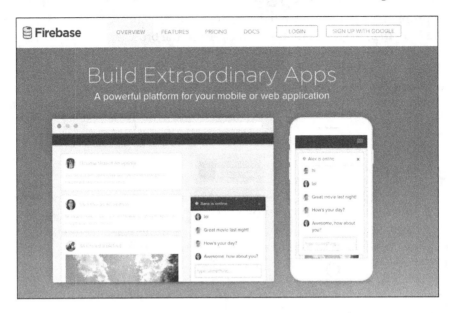

Once this is done, you should see a button labeled **Sign Up With Google** on the top right-hand corner.

When you click this button, you should see a Gmail window asking you to select or log in to a Google account. After you select the Google account you want to use, you should be redirected to your brand new Firebase account. The window you will be redirected to should look like what we have in the following screenshot:

All the examples we have here are based on our sample account. You should not use the URLs from the preceding screenshot but instead use the ones you see in your own window. If you do not, your sample will not work.

You will see that there is a Firebase app created for you called **MY FIRST APP**. When using Firebase, for each app we create we also create an app for it on our Firebase dashboard. This is because Firebase uses a distinct URL to provide you access to the data of each unique application you create. So, think of this **MY FIRST APP** Firebase app as a database.

Now, let's take a closer look at **MY FIRST APP**:

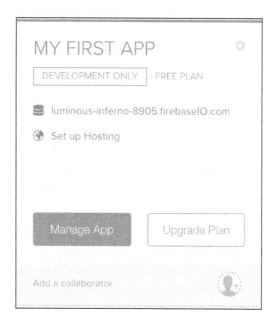

You should see something very similar to the preceding screenshot. You can access the URL for your Firebase database by clicking on the post fixed with the .firebaseIO.com URL. Remember that the URL you see on the screenshots will be different from the ones you see on your dashboard, and you are to use the ones on your dashboard.

You can see that the URL we have here for demonstration is luminous-inferno-8905.firebaseIO.com.

Click the URL you have on your dashboard and that should take you to your Firebase database, which should look similar to the following screenshot:

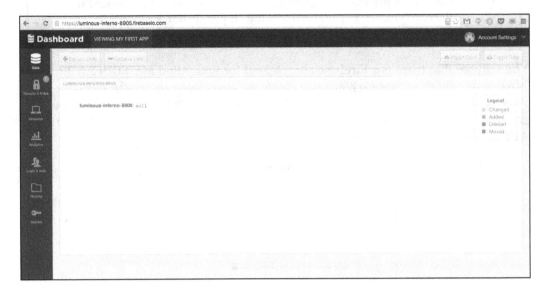

Just to clarify once again, Firebase uses URLs to access databases. What you see in the preceding screenshot is the dashboard for your database. You can also see the same database URL in the browser's address bar. Firebase uses JSON-style data structure, so basically what we send to it is JSON, and what we store is JSON too.

When we add data to our database, we will be able to see it in this dashboard.

Integrate Firebase into tabs-app application

Now that we have our Firebase account and know how to get the URL of our Firebase database, the next step is to integrate it into our application.

Adding Firebase and Angular-Fire scripts

The first thing we need to do is to add the scripts we will need. We will need two scripts. The first is the Firebase library. The second script is the Angular-Fire library. Angular-Fire is an Angular library that makes working with Firebase in an AngularJS application much simpler.

The simplest way is to use the hosted library references. To add this to our app, open your `index.html` file and add the following script references within `<head>` of your application:

```html
<!-- Firebase -->
<script src="https://cdn.firebase.com/js/client/2.2.4/firebase.js"></script>
<!-- AngularFire -->
<script
src="https://cdn.firebase.com/libs/angularfire/1.1.3/
angularfire.min.js"></script>
```

If you have done this correctly, the `head` part of your `index.html` should look like the following screenshot:

```html
<head>
    <meta charset="utf-8">
    <meta name="viewport" content="initial-scale=1, maximum-scale=1, user-scalable=no, width=device-width">
    <title></title>

    <link href="lib/ionic/css/ionic.css" rel="stylesheet">
    <link href="css/style.css" rel="stylesheet">

    <!-- IF using Sass (run gulp sass first), then uncomment below and remove the CSS includes above
    <link href="css/ionic.app.css" rel="stylesheet">
    -->

    <!-- Firebase -->
    <script src="https://cdn.firebase.com/js/client/2.2.4/firebase.js"></script>
    <!-- AngularFire -->
    <script src="https://cdn.firebase.com/libs/angularfire/1.1.3/angularfire.min.js"></script>
    <!-- ionic/angularjs js -->
    <script src="lib/ionic/js/ionic.bundle.js"></script>

    <!-- cordova script (this will be a 404 during development) -->
    <script src="cordova.js"></script>

    <!-- your app's js -->
    <script src="js/app.js"></script>
    <script src="js/controllers.js"></script>
    <script src="js/services.js"></script>
</head>
```

 Make sure your references are below the Ionic bundle as seen in the preceding screenshot. This is very important or else your app will not work properly.

The next step is to reference your Angular-Fire module. This step will ensure that we can use Angular-Fire within our application. The name of this module is `firebase`. This will be added to the root module of your application, called `starter` in your `app.js` file.

Currently, this module's declaration looks something like what we have in the following screenshot:

```
angular.module('starter', ['ionic', 'starter.controllers', 'starter.services'])
```

You will need to add the `firebase` module as a dependent module. Doing this will make the module declaration to look something like what we have in the following screenshot:

```
angular.module('starter', ['ionic', 'starter.controllers', 'starter.services', 'firebase'])
```

You can see that the `firebase` module is now added to the module declaration as a dependency. By doing this, we have successfully integrated Firebase into the skin of our app. The next step is to actually implement it to save our data.

Implementing Firebase to our app

To implement Firebase in our app, we will need to do some work within our `WallController` controller. The first thing we need to code for is the ability to pull items from the database. The second thing we need to code for is the ability to add items to the database.

Pulling from database

The first thing we need to do is to add the `$firebaseArray` service dependency into our `WallController` controller. This service is part of the Angular-Fire library and makes it easy for us to work with arrays in Firebase.

Adding the service dependency correctly should make your `WallController` controller definition look like what we have in the following screenshot:

```
.controller('WallController', function($scope, $firebaseArray) {
```

The next step is to actually write code to pull the data from the database. Replicate the code provided in the following code block in your `WallController` controller:

```
var postsDatabaseRef = new Firebase("https://<YOUR-
FIREBASE-APP>.firebaseio.com").child('posts');
var postsData = $firebaseArray(postsDatabaseRef);
```

This piece of code creates a new Firebase reference at first. We passed in the URL of the Firebase database that we created earlier. Make sure you change the placeholder text (YOUR-FIREBASE-APP) to reflect the URL of your Firebase database.

After this, we used the $firebase service that we added earlier to create a path called postData. The last step we need to do is to allow our app to load data from this postData path and use it. To do this, we need to edit the code of our WallController slightly. Currently, our WallController controller's code looks like what we have in the following screenshot:

```
.controller('WallController', function($scope, $firebaseArray) {
    var postsDatabaseRef = new Firebase("https://<YOUR-FIREBASE-APP>.firebaseio.com");
    var postsData = $firebaseArray(postsDatabaseRef).child('posts');

    $scope.post = {
      message : ''
    };

    $scope.posts = [];

    $scope.addPost = function () {
      $scope.posts.unshift($scope.post);

      $scope.post = {
        message: ''
      };
    };

})
```

Pay close attention to the piece of code highlighted in the preceding screenshot. We need to edit this piece of code such that instead of equating to an empty array, it should equate to our postData variable. Doing this correctly should make us end up with a WallController controller that looks like the following screenshot:

```
.controller('WallController', function($scope, $firebaseArray) {
    var postsDatabaseRef = new Firebase("https://<YOUR-FIREBASE-APP>.firebaseio.com");
    var postsData = $firebaseArray(postsDatabaseRef).child('posts');

    $scope.post = {
      message : ''
    };

    $scope.posts = postsData;

    $scope.addPost = function () {
      $scope.posts.unshift($scope.post);

      $scope.post = {
        message: ''
      };
    };

})
```

By doing this, we have implemented the first part; our Firebase implementation and our app now loads data from our database. The next step is to implement the code to add our posts to our database.

Adding to database

Adding to the database is actually pretty easy. All we need to do is slightly edit our `addPost()` function. Currently, our `addPost()` function looks like what we have in the following screenshot:

```
$scope.addPost = function () {
    $scope.posts.unshift($scope.post);

    $scope.post = {
        message: ''
    };
};
```

To make our data persist in our database, we only need to replace the code highlighted in the preceding screenshot with the following code block:

```
$scope.posts.$add($scope.post);
```

Now, your `addPost()` function should look like what we have in the following screenshot:

```
$scope.addPost = function () {
    $scope.posts.$add($scope.post);

    $scope.post = {
        message: ''
    };
};
```

All we did was just change the `unshift()` method to the `$add()` method. The `$add()` method is a method from Firebase that adds items to a Firebase database. At this point, we have completed the implementation of our backend. As easy as that was, we have a working database in just a few short steps and can now test this live. Your final `WallController` controller should look like the following code block:

```
.controller('WallController', function($scope, $firebaseArray) {
    var postsDatabaseRef = new Firebase("https://<YOUR-FIREBASE-
    APP>.firebaseio.com").child('posts');
    var postsData = $firebaseArray(postsDatabaseRef);

    $scope.post = {
```

```
    message : ''
  };

  $scope.posts = postsData;

  $scope.addPost = function () {
    $scope.posts.$add($scope.post);

    $scope.post = {
      message: ''
    };
  };

})
```

To test your application, simply run your app using the `ionic serve` technique. When you do this, you should be able to enter messages in your application, and even after you refresh your browser, the data that you have already posted will still exist. Also, if you have a look at the Firebase dashboard for your database, you will see that the data you entered in the app is present there.

Summary

In this chapter, we learned some really cool ways of using Firebase to easily add a backend to our Ionic app. We only touched upon what Firebase lets us do, and you can look at the Firebase documentation available at `https://www.firebase.com/docs/` to see the full features of Firebase.

At this point, we have almost come to the end of our book. The next chapter will be the final one, and it is one you should definitely read. It contains some very useful information on how to harness skills learned in this book to get even better at using Ionic.

10
Roundup

In this chapter, we are going to have an overview of the important things that we haven't covered yet about Ionic and which you might find very useful. You will also learn some useful tips about Ionic and discover some great tips about how to make even better use of Ionic to develop great apps.

Uncovered features of Ionic

Although we covered many great topics in this book, there are a lot of great features that we did not cover as they were beyond the scope of this book. We mostly focused on the core features of Ionic, such as how to get Ionic set up. We then learned to create Ionic apps using the blank, side menu, and tabs templates. We also learned to test our Ionic application using the Chrome browser via the `ionic serve` technique.

In this section of the book, I will name a couple of things that will be useful for you to get to grips with in order to become better at Ionic.

Appcamp.IO

`Appcamp.IO` is a free website created by some of the Ionic staff. It is a place where you can go and learn some tips and tricks that will sharpen your Ionic development skills.

The content on `Appcamp.IO` is great for beginners, and it is in some ways in line with the philosophy of this book.

The Ionic documentation

The Ionic documentation page is pretty much the Bible for everything on Ionic. Ionic is very well documented and any feature you want to use is provided there with the sample code and how to use it. You can access the Ionic documentation at `http://www.ionicframework.com/docs`:

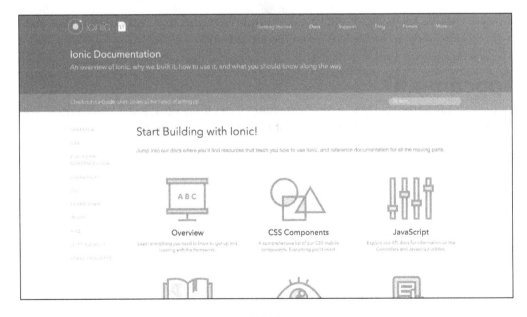

The Ionic creator

This is the drag-and-drop tool built by Ionic for people who want to design their first app or people with limited coding skills. Its greatest feature is that anything you design by dragging and dropping Ionic elements can be tested in the browser, and the code can be extracted as a ready-to-go application. This is great news for designers who don't know how to code as they can quickly use the visual drag-and-drop features of the Ionic creator to design their apps and pass on the code to seasoned developers. You can visit the Ionic creator website at `https://creator.ionic.io`.

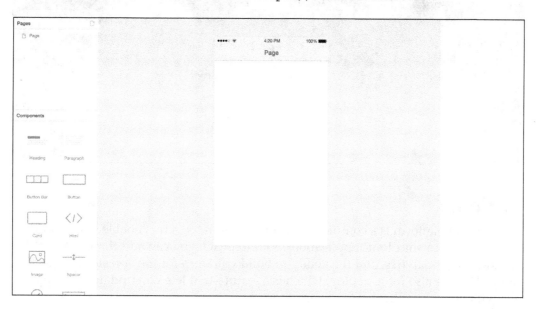

The Ionic code pen

Sometimes, even after you have visited the documentation for some component of Ionic, you will still want to see a real code sample. Or maybe you want to try to reproduce a bug to show others. This is where the Ionic code pen site shines. It is a place where you can find some really great implementations of different features with the code available for you to learn from. It is also the best way to showcase a bug to people who can see it and help you resolve any issues.

You can visit the Ionic code pen website at `http://codepen.ion/ionic`.

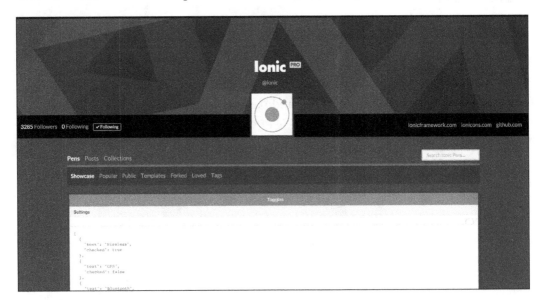

Ionic.IO

The Ionic.IO platform is a complete suite of premium tools that enable you to add great services to your Ionic application. With Ionic.IO, you can add things like **Push Notification**, **Analytics**, and the ability to build your app for the app store in the cloud. There is also Ionic deploy, which is a feature that lets you update your app live without resubmitting it to the app store.

At the time of writing this book, the Ionic.IO tools were all in beta, and although they were free at the time of writing, Ionic has announced that they will be paid services in future. This is something that you should closely follow as you might find yourself needing to use some of the services provided by the Ionic.IO platform.

You can visit the Ionic.IO platform at `http://www.ionic.io`.

The Ionic playground

The Ionic playground is a very new and useful tool to quickly bootstrap an idea. It is a great way to simply spin off code and have it show you the results right there in the browser. I personally see this tool as very useful in the educational world as it makes it easy to create Ionic applications with only a browser.

If you find yourself needing to showcase/demo something quickly without any setup, and have a computer close-by, then make sure you give the Ionic playground a try.

You can visit the Ionic playground at `http://play.ionic.io/`.

The Ionic community

One of the chief reasons Ionic is very successful is the fact that it has a strong active community. From social media and meetup groups to open source activists, Ionic has a wide range of support from people around the world. This means that if you do run into problems of any sort, you are never too far from help. With that in mind, here are some great links to community elements that you might want to keep an eye on:

- **The Ionic forum**: The Ionic forum really is a great place to voice your troubles or find solutions to shared problems. There are multiple active members and users who also get motivational badges for contributing to the forum by commenting and helping others find solutions. You can access this forum at `http://forum.ionicframework.com`.

- **The Ionic Slack channel**: This channel has over 4000 people active on it 24/7 and in multiple countries. It is a great place to meet people, find work, look for help, employ someone, or just simply express yourself. To join the Ionic Slack channel, simply request an invitation for free at `http://ionicworldwide.herokuapp.com`.

- **Twitter**: Twitter is the most vibrant social medium when it comes to finding the latest and greatest thing about Ionic. If you use Twitter, you can follow `@ionicframework` for more information and updates.

- **The Ionic blog**: Ionic writes blog posts very actively about various topics relating to using Ionic. Some of these posts could be about critical updates, inspirational stories, or even announcements of new products or features. You can find the Ionic blog at `http://blog.ionic.io`.

- **Ionic meetup groups**: Around the world, there are hundreds of meetup groups autonomously hosting events and meetups. This is a community effort by local people to grow Ionic awareness in their locality, and you are almost guaranteed to have one in your nearby city. If you do not have one, feel free to start your own local meetup. You can find a list of all meetups at `http://blog.ionic.io/ionic-worldwide`.

The community around Ionic is pretty much the main reason why it grew so rapidly, and you should be sure to trust the community for any needs. As a note, make sure to use the skills you have learned from this book to really strive and improve your Ionic skills and build some great mobile applications. Remember that nothing is too simple to be great and nothing is too great to be too difficult to build.

Useful resources

The following are some useful links to some sites and resources that will aid you further in your quest to learn more about Ionic:

- **The Ionic framework**: `http://www.ionicframework.com`
- **The Ionic GitHub**: `http://www.github.com/driftyco/ionic`
- **AngularJS**: `http://www.angularjs.org`
- **Ionic stack overflow**: `http://stackoverflow.com/questions/tagged/ionic-framework`
- **Firebase**: `http://www.firebase.com`
- **NodeJS**: `http://www.nodejs.org`
- **Bower**: `http://www.bower.io`
- **Gulp**: `http://www.gulpjs.com`
- **Cordova**: `https://cordova.apache.org`
- **Ionic market**: `https://market.ionic.io`
- **ngCordova**: `http://ngcordova.com`
- **Ionic jobs**: `http://jobs.ionic.io`
- **Ionic showcase**: `http://showcase.ionicframework.com`
- **Ionic lab**: `http://lab.ionic.io`

Summary

This chapter was a roundup of Ionic and all its features. I hope you will now know how to build rich features for your mobile applications and have them possess native-like features with the help of Ionic.

Index

Symbols

$ionicConfigProvider
about 81, 93
URL 93
$ionicPopover service
adding 71
code, finishing 72
<ion-tab> element 101, 102

A

abstract state 100
account, Firebase
setting up 115-118
Android 1
Android device
todo app, running 30
Angular code, Bucket-List app
Add button, wiring up 46
controller, binding 46
input box model, binding 46
ion-item, binding 47
text, entering into input box 42
wiring, to UI 46
writing 42
AngularJS
URL 131
Apache Cordova 3, 4
Appcamp.IO 125

B

Bower
URL 131
Bucket-List app
about 33

Angular code, writing 42
breaking down 34
creating 33, 34
overview 34
testing 49
UI, designing 34

C

code pen, Ionic
about 127
URL 127
Continuum 28
Cordova
URL 132

D

data, London Tourist App (LTA)
designing 61, 62
retrieving, with $http service 62-65
wiring up 62
documentation page, Ionic
about 126
URL 126

F

features, Ionic
about 125
Appcamp.IO 125
code pen 127
community 130
CSS 6
documentation page 126
Ionic creator 127
Ionic.IO 128

Thank you for buying
Ionic Framework By Example

About Packt Publishing

Packt, pronounced 'packed', published its first book, *Mastering phpMyAdmin for Effective MySQL Management*, in April 2004, and subsequently continued to specialize in publishing highly focused books on specific technologies and solutions.

Our books and publications share the experiences of your fellow IT professionals in adapting and customizing today's systems, applications, and frameworks. Our solution-based books give you the knowledge and power to customize the software and technologies you're using to get the job done. Packt books are more specific and less general than the IT books you have seen in the past. Our unique business model allows us to bring you more focused information, giving you more of what you need to know, and less of what you don't.

Packt is a modern yet unique publishing company that focuses on producing quality, cutting-edge books for communities of developers, administrators, and newbies alike. For more information, please visit our website at www.packtpub.com.

About Packt Open Source

In 2010, Packt launched two new brands, Packt Open Source and Packt Enterprise, in order to continue its focus on specialization. This book is part of the Packt Open Source brand, home to books published on software built around open source licenses, and offering information to anybody from advanced developers to budding web designers. The Open Source brand also runs Packt's Open Source Royalty Scheme, by which Packt gives a royalty to each open source project about whose software a book is sold.

Writing for Packt

We welcome all inquiries from people who are interested in authoring. Book proposals should be sent to author@packtpub.com. If your book idea is still at an early stage and you would like to discuss it first before writing a formal book proposal, then please contact us; one of our commissioning editors will get in touch with you.

We're not just looking for published authors; if you have strong technical skills but no writing experience, our experienced editors can help you develop a writing career, or simply get some additional reward for your expertise.

Beginning Ionic Hybrid Application Development [Video]

ISBN: 978-1-78528-446-5   Duration: 01:01 hours

Explore Ionic to build elegant, native-looking applications for iOS and Android

1. Get to grips with hybrid mobile application development by calling upon the combined power of Ionic, AngularJS and Cordova.

2. Understand how to utilize AngularJS functions such as controllers, views, and routes.

3. Enhance the user experience by implementing attractive features, such as infinite scrolling, pull-to-refresh, as well as third-party services.

Learning Ionic

ISBN: 978-1-78355-260-3   Paperback: 388 pages

Build real-time and hybrid mobile applications with Ionic

1. Create hybrid mobile applications by combining the capabilities of Ionic, Cordova, and AngularJS.

2. Reduce the time to market your application using Ionic, that helps in rapid application development.

3. Detailed code examples and explanations, helping you get up and running with Ionic quickly and easily.

Please check **www.PacktPub.com** for information on our titles

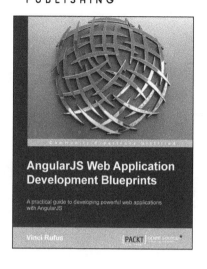

AngularJS Web Application Development Blueprint

ISBN: 978-1-78328-561-7   Paperback: 300 pages

A practical guide to developing powerful web applications with AngularJS

1. Get to grips with AngularJS and the development of single-page web applications.

2. Develop rapid prototypes with ease using Bootstraps Grid system.

3. Complete and in depth tutorials covering many applications.

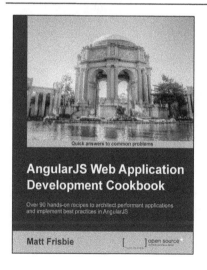

AngularJS Web Application Development Cookbook

ISBN: 978-1-78328-335-4   Paperback: 346 pages

Over 90 hands-on recipes to architect performant applications and implement best practices in AngularJS

1. Understand how to design and organize your AngularJS application to make it efficient, performant, and scalable.

2. Discover patterns and strategies that will give your insights into the best ways to construct production AngularJS applications.

3. Get the most out of AngularJS by gaining exposure to real-world examples.

Please check **www.PacktPub.com** for information on our titles